# YOUTH PROGRAMS FROM
## THE BIBLE

# YOUTH PROGRAMS FROM THE BIBLE

by
B. Hoyt Evans

**BAKER BOOK HOUSE**
Grand Rapids, Michigan

PHOTOLITHOPRINTED BY CUSHING - MALLOY, INC.
ANN ARBOR, MICHIGAN, UNITED STATES OF AMERICA
1 9 6 8

To
My Wife

# Foreword

The purpose of the Bible study programs in this book is to give a survey of the history recorded in the Bible—from creation through the restoration after the Babylonian exile, and from the coming of Christ through the early years of the Church. We should bear in mind, as we study, that the poetical and prophetical books of the Old Testament and the epistles of the New Testament fit into these historical periods. Most important of all, let us remember that the main purpose of any Bible study is to bring us to a better knowledge of Jesus Christ.

# Contents

## NEW TESTAMENT

# 1. The Book of Books

Scripture: Psalm 119:9-16 and II Timothy 3:14-17

Suggested Hymns:

"How Precious Is the Book Divine"
"Wonderful Words of Life"
"Lord, Speak to Me That I May Speak"

*Program Leader's Introduction*
When people call the Bible the "Book of Books," they may mean it in either one of two ways. They may have in mind that the Bible is the greatest of all books, which it is. On the other hand, they may mean that the Bible is made up of many books, which is also true. It is sometimes called the Divine Library. Actually there are sixty-six books in the Bible—thirty-nine in the Old Testament and twenty-seven in the New Testament and these books were written by approximately forty different human authors over a period of fifteen hundred years. In view of these facts, it would be expected that the Bible would be a hopeless confusion and hodgepodge of conflicting ideas and teachings. Surprisingly, this is not the case at all. While there are obvious differences in writing styles, the Bible tells one story—God's story—God is the chief character throughout its pages. The Bible has one theme: God's salvation through Christ. From beginning to end the Bible is God's revelation: of Himself to men, of His plan of salvation through the Divine Redeemer, and of His will for the life of man.

*First Speaker*
The Bible is an authoritative book. We are to believe what it teaches and to obey its commands. The main reason for its authoritative character is that it is God's Word. As we have already been told, the Bible had approximately forty human authors, but its basic author is God. By His Holy Spirit He so guided the human authors that they wrote what He wanted them to write. The Bible has its own definition of inspiration: "For the prophecy came not in old time by the will of man; but holy

men of God spake as they were moved by the Holy Ghost" (II Peter 1:21). The Bible tells us also that because it is inspired it is important to us and reliable: "All Scripture is given by inspiration of God, and is profitable for doctrine, for reproof, for correction, for instruction in righteousness: that the man of God may be perfect, thoroughly furnished unto all good works" (II Timothy 3:16, 17).

One o f the most convincing evidences of the reliability of the Bible is to be found in the attitude of Jesus toward Scripture as recorded in the four Gospels. Not once did He indicate any doubt about the truthfulness of Scripture. As a matter of fact, He quoted from the Old Testament fifty-five times, not counting duplications, and these quotations were taken from every part of the Old Testament. He referred to specific names, places, and incidents, accepting these all as factual. In at least twenty instances He referred to the fulfillment of Scriptural prophecies. He appealed to the Scriptures at least fifteen times in defense of His own statements and actions. On three occasions He affirmed the complete dependability and finality of the Scriptures. An example is: "Scripture cannot be broken" (John 10:35). The other two may be read in Matthew 5:17-18 and Luke 16:17. Someone may object that Jesus had in mind only the Old Testament, but it is obvious from the following passage that New Testament writings were accepted as Scriptural: "Paul also according to the wisdom given unto him hath written unto you; as also in all his epistles, speaking in them of these things; in which are some things hard to be understood, which they that are unlearned and unstable wrest, as they do also the other Scriptures. . ." (II Peter 3:15, 16).

*Second Speaker*

It will help us in our understanding of the Bible if we know how it is organized. The basic divisions are the Old Testament and the New Testament. The Old Testament looks forward to the coming of the Saviour, and the New Testament gives us the record of His coming and an explanation of what His coming means.

The Old Testament has its own organization into divisions. The first of these is made up of the first five books—Genesis through Deuteronomy. These are called the Books of the Law.

Actually they tell of creation and record human history to the time of Abraham and then the history of God's people through the Egyptian captivity and the wilderness wanderings. This division of books gets its name from the laws of God which are recorded in them. God gave three kinds of laws: (1) practical laws, governing food, sanitation, etc.; (2) ceremonial laws, governing feasts, sacrifices, and religious rites; and (3) moral laws, summarized in the Ten Commandments, which are eternally valid standards for human conduct.

The next division is the Books of History including the twelve books, Joshua through Esther. They record the history of God's people from the time of their entrance into the promised land, through the period of the Judges, the united kingdom, the divided kingdom, the captivity, and the restoration of Jerusalem. In these records we see the sinfulness of the people and the justice, faithfulness, and mercy of God.

The Books of Poetry—Job, Psalms, Proverbs, Ecclesiastes, and The Song of Solomon—are found in the middle of the Old Testament. Several human authors contributed to these beautiful words of wisdom and inspiration, but the chief contributors were David and Solomon. These writings came from several centuries before and after the time of David and Solomon.

The last seventeen books of the Old Testament are the prophecies. The first of these—Isaiah, Jeremiah, Ezekiel, and Daniel—are referred to as Major Prophets, not because they were necessarily more important, but because their writings were longer. These prophets, major and minor, served from the time of the Kingdoms through the exile and into the period of restoration. They served as God's messengers to the people: speaking of the Saviour to come, of judgment, of righteous living, of God's mercy, and of future hope.

*Third Speaker*

The first division of the New Testament is the four Gospels. The Gospels tell of the birth, life, ministry, death, and resurrection of Christ, but they cannot properly be called biographies. They do more than tell the life of Christ from their different points of view—they seek to present Christ as God and Saviour and to call for a verdict from their readers. A clear example of this is found in John 20:30, 31: "And many other signs truly did

Jesus in the presence of His disciples, which are not written in this book; but these are written, that ye might believe that Jesus is the Christ, the Son of God; and that believing, ye might have life through his name."

The next division of the New Testament is just one book, the Book of Acts. It records the history of the Holy Spirit's work in the early years of the Christian church.

The New Testament Epistles were letters, written by Paul and others to individuals and churches during the first Christian century. These letters instruct, admonish, correct, and commend the people and churches to whom they are written according to the will of God. Their teachings are of abiding value to the church today.

The last book of the New Testament, the Book of Revelation, is very unique. In language rich in imagery and mystery it speaks of things that were, things that are, and things that are to come. It describes the final victory of God's Kingdom and the blessedness of those who put their trust in Christ.

*Program Leader*

The purpose of the Bible study programs in this book is to give a survey of the history recorded in the Bible—from creation through the restoration after the exile and from the coming of Christ through the early years of the church. Let us remember, as we study, that the Poetry and Prophets of the Old Testament and the Epistles of the New Testament fit into these historical periods. Most important of all, let us remember that the main purpose of any Bible study is to bring us to a better knowledge of Jesus Christ.

(Closing Prayer)

# 2. A Book of Beginnings

Scripture: John 1:1-14

Suggested Hymns:

"I Sing the Mighty Power of God"
"O Worship the King"
"God That Madest Earth and Heaven"

*Suggestions to Program Leader*

(If possible, ask the young people to read the first five chapters of Genesis before they come to the meeting. Also, ask them to bring their Bibles. Provide extra Bibles for those who may not have their own. Have a prayer or series of prayers for God's guidance before you begin the time of study. If you have a large number of young people, divide into three groups and assign one of the passages and accompanying questions listed below to each group. Let each group answer the questions from their Bibles, and then reassemble and report their findings. If your organization is not large enough to divide, let the whole number study all of the questions and answer them. Whether you divide into groups or not, allow time for discussion as the questions are answered. You may want to ask your minister or adult advisor to sum up the ideas at the conclusion of the program.)

*Program Leader's Introduction*

The word "genesis" means beginning. Genesis is indeed an appropriate title for the first book of the Bible. It records the beginnings of a great many things. It does not, however, tell about the beginning of God because God has no beginning. He was present at the beginning of all other things. In fact, He is the beginner.

In this program we shall be studying the first five chapters of Genesis. In these chapters we shall learn of the beginning of the universe and of human history; the beginning of sin and its consequences; and the beginning of our present pattern of living.

*The Beginnings of the Universe and of Human History,* Chapters
1 and 2
 1. What is the difference between the words "created" and
    "made"? For a definition of "create" see Hebrews 11:3.
 2. How does the Bible account for the existence of the material
    universe, biological life, and the human soul? (Genesis 1:1,
    21, 27; 2:7).
 3. What did God create on each day? What significance do you
    see in this order?
 4. Where do you find the beginning of Sabbath observance?
 5. What is the relation of man to the remainder of creation?
    (Genesis 1:26-30; 2:15-16; Psalm 8:4-8).
 6. Where is the beginning of marriage and what is its ideal?

*The Beginning of Sin and Its Consequences,* Chapter 3
 1. What does the serpent's question (3:1) insinuate?
 2. Of what does the serpent accuse God in verses 4 and 5?
 3. Does temptation often begin with doubt? What were Adam
    and Eve's doubts about God?
 4. What were the real reasons for their being afraid (vs. 10)
    since they had not been afraid of God's presence before?
 5. Was Adam justified in trying to shift the blame to Eve?
    Why, or why not?
 6. What promise of hope is suggested in 3:15? In whom was
    this promise truly fulfilled?
 7. What blessings and privileges were lost by man through his
    disobedience? His relation to God?

*The Beginnings of Our Present Pattern of Life,* Chapters 4 and 5
 1. Why was Cain's offering not accepted? (Genesis 4:7; He-
    brews 11:4)
 2. What is the Christian answer to Cain's question in 4:9?
 3. What does it mean that "Cain went out [away] from the
    presence of the Lord"?
 4. Through whom was a new line of inheritance established for
    the fulfillment of the promise in 3:15? (Genesis 4:25-16;
    5:3; Luke 3:38)
 5. Point out the beginnings of selfishness, vengeance, commu-
    nity living, fine arts, and mechanical skills. (Genesis 4:20-24)
 6. What does it mean that Enoch "walked with God" and "he

was not, for God took him"? Do you see anything of faith and grace here? (See Hebrews 11:5)

*Program Leader*

We hardly begin our study of the first book of the Bible until we come to the tragedy of human sin and failure. If our God were not a God of grace and mercy, the Bible could very well have ended with the third chapter of Genesis, and the events recorded there could have included the end as well as the beginning of human history. How thankful we should be that our God loves us and has provided a way of salvation from sin and death!

(Closing Prayer)

# 3. Three Structures

Scripture: Psalm 96

Suggested Hymns:

"Come, Thou Fount of Every Blessing"
"God Will Take Care of You"
"Rescue the Perishing"

*Suggestions for Program Leader*
(We have another study of Genesis, this time in the form of a panel discussion. Have three or four members on the panel plus a moderator. Ask all panel members to read carefully Genesis 6-11 before program time. Have them bring their Bibles. Supply Bibles for the other young people so they can follow along during the study. Address the questions to the panel members, taking turns. After the person who is asked the question has opportunity to give his answer, let the other panel members make additional comments. It is understood that the panel members may use their Bibles during the program.)

*Moderator's Introduction*
The section of Genesis we are studying today tells of the building of three structures: an ark, an altar, and a tower. We shall study the passage by putting questions to the panel for their answers and comments. We are asking all of you to open your Bibles to Genesis 6-11 and follow the discussion. As the study proceeds, ask yourself what was the purpose of the ark, the altar, and the tower of Babel.

## Questions for Study and Discussion

1. What was the reason for the flood? (Genesis 6:5-7, 11-13)
2. What is the significance of the words "every," "only," and "continually" in Genesis 6:5?
3. In what sense was Noah a "just [righteous] man and perfect [blameless] in his generations"? (Genesis 6:9 and Hebrews 11:7)

4. If a cubit is eighteen inches, what were the approximate dimensions of the ark?

5. Who were the passengers in the ark and what provision was made for their nourishment?

6. How did Noah demonstrate his faith? (Genesis 6:22; 7:5)

7. How long did it rain, and how long did the flood waters "prevail"?

8. What do you understand by "fountain of the deep"? (Genesis 7:11 and 8:2)

9. What was the first thing Noah did upon coming out of the ark? (Genesis 8:20)

10. What promise did God make, and what was its sign? (Genesis 8:21, 22; 9:9-16)

11. What task was given to Noah and his descendants, and what provision was made for them? (Genesis 9:1-4)

12. What is the reason for the sacredness of human life, and what is the punishment for murder? (Genesis 9:5, 6)

13. How does the life of Noah demonstrate that a man may resist great temptations and yet stumble before small ones? (Genesis 9:21)

14. Describe the contrasting attitudes of Noah's sons toward his sin and shame.

15. From which son of Noah were the Hebrews descended?

16. How was the dividing of these families into nations a part of God's purpose as stated in Genesis 9:1?

17. What was the nature of the rebellion and disobedience symbolized in the building of the tower of Babel?

18. Who directed the building of the ark? The altar? The tower? Who actually built each? What were their purposes?

19. In what ways was the ark a type of the salvation of Christ?

*Program Leader*

Again, at the time of Noah, God would have been justified in bringing the human race to an end because of the sinfulness of mankind, but He did not. The fact that He did not is proof to us that He is a God of grace and mercy. "He hath not dealt with us after our sins, nor rewarded us according to our iniquities" (Psalm 103:10). He continues to be a merciful God, and we experience His mercy in Jesus Christ. Many people still try to live their lives without God, like the people of Babel. For those who will trust in God, there is still salvation even as He provided safety in the ark for Noah and his family. Those of us who have accepted Christ as Saviour will naturally want to show our gratitude in worship just as Noah did when he came out of the ark.

(Closing Prayer)

# 4. The Father of the Faithful

Scripture: Hebrews 11:8-19

Suggested Hymns:

"Anywhere with Jesus I Can Safely Go"
"He Leadeth Me, O Blessed Thought"
"My Faith Looks Up to Thee"

*Program Leader's Introduction*

Abraham is easily one of the greatest characters in the Bible. We will notice that the movement of the book of Genesis slows down when it comes to him. The first eleven chapters of the book cover centuries of time, but when we come to Abraham, the record goes into great detail. This indicates his place of importance in the story which the Bible is telling.

We shall study what the Bible says about Abraham and his place in God's plan by answering from our Bibles the questions which I shall read. First, I shall read the question and then give the chapter and verse references where the answer may be found. When you have located the answer, raise your hand, and I shall call on you to give it. (Write the answers on the board as they are given. Keep calling on different persons until the answers are correct and complete. Allow time for discussion, and be sure that all the young people have Bibles.)

## Questions for Study and Discussion

1. What difficult act of separation did God call on Abraham to make? (Genesis 12:1; Hebrews 11:8)
2. What did God promise Abraham as a reward for his faith and obedience? (Genesis 12:2, 3)
3. Of what unusual deception was Abraham guilty on two different occasions? (Genesis 12:11-20; 20:1-13)
4. Why was Lot's decision to settle in the plains of Jordan not a wise one? (Genesis 13:12, 13)
5. Who was Melchizedek and whom did he foreshadow? (Genesis 14:18-20; Hebrews 7:1-3; 14-17)

6. What made Abraham really acceptable before God? (Genesis 15:6; Romans 4:3-5)
7. Who was Hagar? Who was Ishmael? Was it God's plan that His promise to Abraham should be fulfilled through the son of Hagar? (Genesis 16:1-3; 15, 16; Galatians 4:22, 23)
8. What promise did God make concerning Ishmael? (Genesis 17:20)
9. How many times did Abraham pray for the people of Sodom? (Genesis 18:23-32)
10. What was the fate of Lot's wife and why? (Genesis 19:17, 26)
11. How did Lot benefit by Abraham's faith and prayers? (Genesis 19:29)
12. How old were Sarah and Abraham when Isaac was born? (Genesis 17:17; 21:5)
13. How was God's promise to Abraham concerning Ishmael fulfilled? (Genesis 21:17-21)
14. How does Genesis 22:8 suggest the salvation which God provides through Christ?
15. What made Abraham willing to offer Isaac as a sacrifice? (Hebrews 11:17-19)
16. In what sense can Gentile Christians be called the descendents of Abraham? (Galatians 3:6-14, 29)

(Closing Prayer)

# 5. A Passive Father and Strong Sons

Scripture: Psalm 1

Suggested Hymns:

"O God of Bethel, by Whose Hand"
"O Jesus, I Have Promised"
"Just As I Am"

*Suggestions to Program Leader*
(This is another program making use of a discussion panel. Choose the panel members and ask them to read carefully Genesis 24-36. Have all the young people bring their Bibles. Give the questions to the panel members in turn. After the person questioned has had opportunity to give his answer, let the other members comment. Also, invite comments and questions from the audience. Ask the minister and/or adult advisor to be on hand as a resource person.)

*Panel Moderator's Introduction*
It is sometimes said that Isaac was the weak son of a strong father and the weak father of two strong sons. Such a judgment of Isaac is in all probability far too harsh. Even so, he was certainly not as colorful as his father and his sons. He was a passive personality—one who seemed often to be controlled by circumstances, while his father and sons seemed to be in control of things themselves. Nevertheless, Isaac had an important place in God's plan. It ought to encourage all of us who are ordinary people to know that God used an ordinary person like Isaac as well as his more illustrious relatives.

## Questions for Study and Discussion

1. Why do you suppose Abraham did not want Isaac to take a wife from among the Canaanites?
2. What were the signs that the Lord had led Abraham's servant to Rebekah? (Genesis 24:12-27; 42-48)
3. Considering the fact that a birthright had spiritual value

and significance what would you say about Esau's spirituality? (Genesis 25:29-34)

4. What sin of Abraham did Isaac repeat? (Genesis 26:1-11)

5. Why were Esau's wives a disappointment to Isaac and Rebekah? (Genesis 26:34, 35)

6. How did Jacob manage to deceive his father and steal his brother's blessing? (Genesis 27)

7. Why was it necessary for Jacob to leave home? (Genesis 27:41-45; 28:1, 2)

8. What vision did Jacob see at Bethel and what promise was repeated to him? (Genesis 28:11-15)

9. Where in Genesis 28 do you find an instance of the tithe?

10. How was Jacob, the deceiver, deceived? (Genesis 29:15-25)

11. What indication is there that Laban was a spiritual parasite —one who sought what benefit he could from the Lord's blessings to others without serving the Lord himself? (Genesis 30:27)

12. Was Jacob taking what really did not belong to him when he took his family and flocks and left Laban? (Genesis 31:36-42) Why or why not?

13. What was Jacob's strategy in preparing to meet Esau? (Genesis 32:7, 8)

14. How did the Lord break Jacob's attitude of proud self-sufficiency? (Genesis 32:24, 25)

15. What was Jacob's new name and what did it mean? (Genesis 32:28)

16. What was the nature of the reunion of Jacob and Esau? (Genesis 33:4, 8-10)

17. How had God moved in the intervening years to fulfill the promise (Genesis 28:14, 15) He had made to Jacob at Bethel years before?

18. Which of Israel's sons would establish the line through which the Saviour would be born? (Micah 5:2; Matthew 2:5, 6)

*Program Leader*

Isaac is said to have been a mild man—even a weak man. A society which admires activity and praises ambition is not likely to appreciate him. His sons were more active and ambitious, but their activity and ambition often became snares to them. The ideal attitude is to be as submissive to God's will as Isaac was when Abraham prepared to offer him as a sacrifice and to be as enthusiastic about serving the Lord as Jacob was enthusiastic about making a name for himself.

(Closing Prayer)

# 6. God's Governor in Egypt

Scripture: Psalm 37:1-9

Suggested Hymns:

> "Yield Not to Temptation"
> "I Would Be True"
> "My Times Are in Thy Hands"

*Suggestions to Program Leader*

(This is to be a quiz program. Ask all the young people to read Genesis 37-50 before coming to the program—a good way to spend part of Sunday afternoon. If possible, have these questions mimeographed, leaving space on the paper for answers. If this is not possible, you can write the questions on the blackboard or on a large sheet of paper. If you cannot do this, then read them out slowly and distinctly. Have the young people answer as many as they can without referring to their Bibles. Then correct the wrong answers and supply the missing ones by looking up the references in your Bibles.)

1.  What father was guilty of unwise favoritism? (37:3) (All references in this set of questions are in Genesis.)
2.  Who was hated for his dreams? (37:5)
3.  For whom did the "sun, moon, and eleven stars" stand? (37: 10)
4.  Where did Joseph find his brothers when sent to look for them by Jacob? (37:17)
5.  Which of the brothers spared Joseph's life? (37:21)
6.  To whom did the brothers sell Joseph? (37:28)
7.  What did the brothers lead Jacob to believe had become of Joseph? (37:33)
8.  To whom was Joseph sold in Egypt, and what was his position? (37:36)
9.  Who tried to persuade Joseph to sin? (39:7-12)
10. Who was with Joseph in prison to care for him, and what was his (Joseph's) position there? (39:21-23)

11. Who were the two men who had dreams in the prison? (40:5)
12. What did Pharaoh see in his dream? (41:1-7)
13. Who did Joseph say could give Pharaoh an answer? (41:16)
14. Who was Joseph's wife? (41:45)
15. Who were Joseph's sons? (41:51, 52)
16. Which son did Jacob keep at home when he sent the brothers to Egypt for food? (42:4)
17. What did Joseph accuse his brothers of being? (42:9)
18. Which of the brothers did Joseph keep as a prisoner after their first visit? (42:24)
19. Which brother was responsible for the safety of Benjamin on the second visit? (43:8)
20. In whose sack was Joseph's silver cup found? (44:12)
21. What did Judah propose in order to bring about Benjamin's release? (44:33)
22. According to Joseph, what was God's good purpose and the brother's evil purpose in his coming to Egypt? (45:5; 50:20)
23. What promise did God repeat again to Israel? (46:3)
24. Where in Egypt did the Israelites dwell? (46:28, 34)
25. Where was Israel buried? (50:13)

*Program Leader*

The word "genesis" means beginning. In our study of this book we have learned about the beginning of the material and spiritual universe, the beginning of human life, the beginning of sin, the beginning again after the flood, and the beginning of the human family through which God's Saviour would be born. It is wonderful to see how God overrules the evil intentions and actions of men to work out His will for our good and His glory.

(Closing Prayer)

# 7. The Birth, Preparation, and Call of Moses

Scripture: Exodus 3:1-14

Suggested Hymns:

"O Worship the King"
"Jesus Calls Us: O'er the Tumult"
"Seal Us, O Holy Spirit"

*Suggestions to Program Leader*

(Conduct this program as a panel discussion. Have a panel of at least three persons plus a leader or moderator. Ask the minister or adult advisor to be on hand as a resource person to help with difficult questions. The panel members will use their Bibles during the program, but should have studied Exodus 1-4 and the questions below before coming to the meeting. Address questions to the panel members in turn, and then give the other two members opportunity to add their comments. Ask the other young people to follow the discussion in their Bibles. You may give them opportunities for questions and their comments, if you so desire.)

*Program Leader's Introduction*

The Book of Exodus records God's deliverance of His chosen people, the children of Israel, from their bondage in Egypt. It also tells of His wonderful provisions for their establishment as a nation. Our program today deals mainly with the man whom God called to lead His people from slavery into the land He had promised them. We shall be studying the birth, call, and preparation of Moses. Our panel members (call them by name) have studied the appropriate chapters of Exodus, and are prepared to discuss our questions. We hope all of you will follow the discussion very carefully in your Bibles.

## Questions for Study and Discussion

1. What does it mean that the new king of Egypt "knew not [did not know] Joseph"? (1:8)

2. What evidences of fear, suspicion, and resentment do you find in the words of the king? (1:9-10)
3. Was the king merely interested in controlling the Israelites, or did he actually want to exterminate them? Explain your answer.
4. How did the midwives frustrate the king's plan?
5. Trace the steps in the daring plan of Moses' mother to save her son. (2:3-7)
6. Exodus 2:11-12 is said to have been a point of decision. What was the decision? (See Hebrews 11:24-26.)
7. What is symbolized in the bush that was burned but not consumed? (3:2)
8. What act of reverence did God require? (3:5)
9. How did God identify Himself with the history of Israel? (3:6)
10. What was God's declared purpose at this time? (3:8)
11. What excuses did Moses offer? (3:13; 4:1; 4:10)
12. What miraculous signs of His power and presence did God give to Moses? (4:2-9)
13. Who was to be Moses' spokesman?
14. How do you think Moses' life as a prince in Egypt prepared him for the work to which God called him?
15. Do you think the years Moses spent in Midian were wasted as far as preparation for his calling was concerned? Why or why not?
16. What was the response of the people to the words and signs of the Lord given through Aaron and Moses? (4:31)

*Program Leader*

Time and time again at critical points in history God has raised up men to do some particular work to the glory of His name. Moses was such a man. When we look at the whole story of his life, we can see how God was giving him special preparation for the most difficult and important task of leading the Israelites to freedom. The life of Moses is one of many illustrations in the Bible of God's wise and loving providence.

(Closing Prayer)

# 8. The Might of God in Egypt

Scripture: Exodus 12:1-14

Suggested Hymns:

> "Come, Thou Almighty King"
> "Stand Up for Jesus"
> "Rise Up, O Men of God"

## Suggestions to Program Leader

(Ask the young people to read Exodus 5-12 before coming to the meeting. Urge them to bring their own Bibles, but provide extra copies for those who do not have their own. Write the twelve questions given below where all can see them. Put them on a chalkboard or large piece of paper. Distribute papers and pencils and ask the young people to write out answers to the questions, using their Bibles. When all have completed their answers, read the questions aloud, one by one, and compare the answers. Ask your minister or some other Bible authority to be present.)

## Program Leader's Introduction

When you think about what God called Moses to do, you can understand why he was hesitant to undertake the task. Pharaoh had a valuable supply of cheap labor in the Hebrew slaves, and he would certainly not want to set them free without a struggle. The Hebrews themselves were neither trained nor equipped to fight for their freedom even if they had been anxious to do so.

Even if these slaves could have been set free, which was very unlikely, where could provisions be found to supply them until they could move to the land of promise? How could such an irresponsible, undisciplined group be organized into a nation? Surely the task seemed impossible, but it *was* accomplished through the mighty working of the power of God. In this program we shall be studying the working of God's power in Egypt to bring about the deliverance of His people.

*Questions for Study and Discussion*

1. How did Pharaoh show his contempt for God? (5:2)
2. What was the result of Moses' first request for the release of the Hebrews? (5:6-9)
3. How did the Hebrews react to the increased requirements. (5:20-21) Do you think the increased hardships made the people more anxious to leave Egypt?
4. How did Pharaoh's stubbornness make possible a greater display of God's power in Egypt? (7:3-5)
5. How old were Moses and Aaron? (7:7)
6. How does the incident recorded in 7:12 show the superiority of the power of God over the power of evil?
7. List the ten plagues in order.
8. Was Pharaoh's repentance mentioned in 9:27-28 and 10:16-17 genuine? How do you know?
9. Were Pharaoh's servants as stubborn as he? (10:7)
10. The word translated "borrow" in 11:2 and 12:35 means "ask," so God was not instructing the Hebrews to deceive the Egyptians. The Egyptians gave knowingly. Do you think this was one of the ways God provided for the material needs of His people and for the finery to be used in the tabernacle?
11. What are the similarities and differences between the Passover and the Lord's Supper? (Compare Exodus 12:1-14 and Luke 22:7-20.)
12. Did Pharaoh finally believe that the power of God was superior to all the might of Egypt? Why?

*Program Leader*

The demonstration of God's power was necessary to convince Pharaoh to release the Israelites. It was equally necessary for the sake of the Israelites themselves in order that their faith in the power and purpose of God might be fully established.

(Closing Prayer)

# 9. God Is a Guard and Guide

Scripture: Exodus 15:1-19

Suggested Hymns:

"My Hope Is Built on Nothing Less"
"My Faith Looks Up to Thee"
"He Leadeth Me, O Blessed Thought"

*Suggestions to Program Leader*

(See that all the young people are supplied with Bibles, preferably their own. If possible, have them read Exodus 13-19 before coming to the meeting. Read the questions one by one, giving the reference for the answer where it is supplied. Ask the young people to find the answers in their Bibles and then to volunteer them orally. If the young people do not volunteer the answers readily, you may call on individuals to give their findings. Allow time for discussion between questions, but do not let the program drag.)

*Program Leader's Introduction*

The incidents recorded in the passages we shall be studying in this program illustrate both the changeableness of the human mind and heart and the faithfulness and patience of God. While the Israelites were in Egypt they complained that God had forgotten them. When He did bring about their deliverance in such a wonderful way, they complained of the hardships in the wilderness and longed to be back in Egypt. Are we ever discontented and inconsistent in similar ways? Have you ever heard young people complain because they could not afford to go to college, and then when the way was opened up did not some of them complain because college work was so hard? In these chapters of Exodus (13-19) we shall see God's wise and patient dealings with some unruly, unappreciative people.

## Questions for Study and Discussion

1. Why did God not lead the Israelites through the land of the Philistines, which was the most direct way? (13:17)

2. How did God symbolize His presence and guide the people on their journey? (13:20-22)

3. For what reasons did Pharaoh change his mind and decide to pursue the Israelites? (14:4-5)

4. What evidence is there that the Israelites lost faith in God's power to deliver? (14:10-12)

5. Did the people's deliverance at this time depend in any way on their own efforts? (14:13-14)

6. How did God divide the waters of the Red Sea? (14:21)

7. What effect did the miraculous deliverance have on the hearts of the people? (14:31)

8. What tribes and nations would learn to have fear of and respect for the Lord? (15:14-15)

9. What were the four conditions mentioned in 15:26 for receiving the Lord's blessing and protection?

10. Why did the people murmur against Moses, Aaron, and God? (16:2-3) Did they seem to be more interested in food or freedom?

11. In the giving of bread from Heaven, how did God provide for the keeping of the Sabbath day? (16:5; 26-30)

12. What happened when the people gathered too much manna and tried to keep it over for the next day, with the exception of the Sabbath? (16:16-20)

13. Who led the army of Israel in the fight against Amalek? (Chap. 17)

14. What was Jethro's opinion of God? (18:11-12)

15. What advice did Jethro give Moses? (18:13-26)

16. What did God require of the people and what did He promise them? (19:5-6)

17. What were the visible signs of the majesty of the Lord mentioned in 19:16?

*Program Leader*

Let us recognize God's goodness to us, remembering that He does for us that which is best even if we cannot understand His purposes. It is indeed fortunate that our lives and ways are not determined by our own shortsighted desires, but by the hand of a wise, powerful, and loving God.

(Closing Prayer)

# 10. Laws for God's People

Scripture: Exodus 20:1-17

Suggested Hymns:

"Trust and Obey"
"Who Is On the Lord's Side?"
"O Jesus, I Have Promised"

## Suggestions to Program Leader

(This program on the Ten Commandments seeks to make practical applications of the commandments to the lives of modern young people. It is suggested that you conduct the program as a panel discussion of which you will be the moderator. Choose three or four young people to serve as panel members. Address the questions to them in turn. After the person questioned has given his response, invite the other members of the panel to make their comments. All the young people, panel members and those in the audience alike, should have and use their Bibles.)

## Program Leader's Introduction

There are three types of laws in the Old Testament: (1) Practical laws of everyday living, such as the laws governing sanitation; (2) The ceremonial laws governing feasts, sacrifices, and other religious rites; and (3) The moral law which we find in condensed form in the Ten Commandments. The first two types of laws were temporary in their design. The practical laws applied to definite times and situations, and consequently, the restrictions on diet and sanitation are no longer in effect. The ceremonial laws were in effect until the time of Christ's sacrifice on the cross, but His atoning work brought an end to priesthood, sacrifices, and the ceremonial law. The moral law, however, is an eternally valid guide for conduct and character and has an abiding value.

The moral law, which is so wonderfully summarized in the Ten Commandments, is grounded in the character of God. Man was created in God's image, and the ideal is for him to be like God. The moral law is a standard for the God-like life. No one is saved by keeping it, because no one can keep it. The only person who ever obeyed the moral law perfectly was Christ himself. The high demands of the law and the impossibility of meeting its demands make us see our need of a Saviour. The law also serves as a guide for the proper living of the Christian life.

## Questions for Study and Discussion

1. Why is it necessary to worship God?
2. What are some of the things in these times which young people are tempted to worship and serve in place of God?
3. Why is it wrong to make an image of God?
4. Why is it impossible for any image or picture to show us what God is really like?
5. What is the danger in trying to worship God by means of images?
6. What other things are involved in the Third Commandment besides cursing, swearing, and profane language?
7. What does it mean to "keep the Sabbath day holy"?
8. What are some of the things people commonly do today that violate the Fourth Commandment?
9. Do you think the Fifth Commandment implies that honor should be given to people other than parents? If so, who are they?
10. Keeping the Fifth Commandment should make for a well-ordered home. Why is a well-ordered home more likely to have the blessings promised in the commandment?
11. If the Sixth Commandment requires respect for human life, what does this have to say about the importance of safe driving?
12. What does the Sixth Commandment require with respect to our own personal health habits?
13. If the Seventh Commandment requires us to respect human character, what does this say about our attitudes toward boys and girls we date?
14. What bearing does the Seventh Commandment have on what we read, the movies we see, and the jokes we tell?
15. What does the Eighth Commandment have to say, at least

by implication, about the right of an individual to own property?

16. What are some of the ways the Eighth Commandment can be broken other than by outright stealing?

17. Does the Ninth Commandment safeguard personal reputation? How?

18. What are some of the ways of damaging the reputation of another other than telling an intentional untruth about him?

19. The Tenth Commandment has been called the most spiritual of the commandments. What are the reasons for this?

20. What are some of the other sins to which covetousness could easily lead?

*Program Leader*

At the time when Jesus lived on earth in the flesh it was the custom to interpret the commandments very literally. For instance, a man was judged innocent of breaking the Sixth Commandment unless he had actually murdered someone. Jesus looked behind the overt act to the attitude. He said a man was guilty if he hated his brother. In applying the commandments to our lives today we are likely to make the same mistake—that of being too literal in our interpretations. We need to discover the principles behind the commandments and then to examine our motives and attitudes as well as our deeds.

(Closing Prayer)

# 11. Worship and Work in the Wilderness

Scripture: Exodus 34:1-17

Suggested Hymns:

> "Come, Thou Fount of Every Blessing"
> "Saviour, Like a Shepherd Lead Us"
> "Lead On, O King Eternal"

*Suggestions to Program Leader*
(Look up answers to all the questions and write them out before undertaking to lead this program. See that all the young people are supplied with Bibles. Read the questions one by one, giving the references, and let the young people find the answers in their Bibles. You may assign definite questions to definite individuals, or you may give the the questions to the whole group and then recognize the first person who locates the answer. Do not rush through the questions, but allow time for comments and discussion after each one.)

*Program Leader's Introduction*
The last half of the Book of Exodus describes the organization of the Israelites into a nation. The first forty years of their new independent national life was to be spent in the wilderness. The organization outlined in these twenty chapters especially fitted them for living in the wilderness. There were specific laws concerning personal and property rights. These were based on the principles of the Ten Commandments. There were also specific laws concerning Sabbath observance.

The greater part of this section of Exodus, however, tells of provisions that were made for worshipping God. There is a record of the specifications for and the building of the tabernacle and its furnishings. The tabernacle was a beautiful and costly tent of worship that could be moved from place to place as the people traveled toward the land of promise. There is also a record of the setting aside of the family of Aaron to the office of the priesthood together with a description of their apparel and of their priestly duties. There is also, in these chapters, an account of the serious sin of the people and their punishment by God.

*Questions for Study and Discussion*

1.  How is the seriousness of conscious negligence recognized in 21:29, 36?

2.  What does 23:8 have to say about bribery?

3.  What three times in the year were feasts to the Lord to be kept? (23:14-16)

4.  In what spirit were gifts to the tabernacle to be made? (25:2)

5.  Did God live in the tabernacle only, or also among the people? (25:8)

6.  Who gave the directions for the building of the ark and tabernacle? (25:9)

7.  Who were the first five priests? (28:1)

8.  How do Aaron's duties, described in 28:30, suggest the work of Christ?

9.  How does 30:15 indicate that all souls are of equal value?

10.  What were the priests required to do before they handled holy things? (30:18-21)

11.  Was the work of the craftsmen a "spiritual" service? Why? (31:3)

12.  Did Sabbath observance show a special relationship between the people and God? (31:16-17)

13.  How did Aaron show himself to be a poor leader? (32:1-5)

14.  What do you think of Aaron's excuse? (32:24) Was he telling the truth? Compare his statement with 32:4.

15.  What two lines of reasoning did Moses use in pleading with God to spare Israel? (32:12-13)

16.  Name five conditions the people were to fulfill in order to receive the blessings of the Lord. (34:10-17).

17.  What happened to Moses' physical appearance as a result of his intimate fellowship with God? (34:29-35)

18.  Did the beautiful garments Aaron wore indicate his own personal importance or the importance of his office? (39:1)

19.  What was Moses' estimate of the work of the people, and what did he do? (39:42-43)

20.  How did God indicate His approval of the tabernacle? (40:34)

*Program Leader*

The experiences of God's people in the wilderness give us a typical sample of life with the Lord. There was work and worship, sin and suffering, but, most important of all, there was the loving provision of the powerful God and His gracious and merciful dealings with His faithless, sinful people. We still have the same problems, and He is still the same kind of God.

(Closing Prayer)

# 12. The Taking of the Promised Land

Scripture: Joshua 1:1-9

Suggested Hymns:

> "My Hope Is Built on Nothing Less"
> "Give of Your Best to the Master"
> "Onward, Christian Soldiers"

*Note to Program Leader*

(This is the first of two Bible study programs on the Book of Joshua. We are suggesting the same procedure for both programs. Ask the young people to read the appropriate passages before coming to the meetings—Chapters 1-12 for the first program and Chapters 13-24 for the second program. Request them to bring their own Bibles, but have extra copies for those who may forget. Copy the questions where all can see them. Distribute paper and pencils and have the young people find the answers in their Bibles and write them out. When they have finished writing, compare the answers and discuss them.)

*Program Leader's Introduction*

Joshua was truly a great man. The record of Israel's conquest of the land of Caanan is very largely a record of Joshua's wise and courageous leadership of the people of Israel. He did not pretend to have all the abilities that Moses had, but the abilities he had were important and he used them well. Without a doubt, the most important quality in the life of this man was his strong, humble faith in God. With a wonderful consistency he trusted in the Lord and gave Him the glory for all his successes. With the same consistency he urged his people to put their trust in God. As we study these first twelve chapters of the book, recording the conquest of the land of promise, let us notice especially Joshua's loyalty to the Lord.

## Questions for Study

1. What was the "book of the law" mentioned in 1:8? According to this verse, what were the two main duties of the people with regard to the book?

2. How did Rahab prove her faith in the God of Israel? (Chap. 2)

3. By what sign was Rahab's house to be marked so it would be spared when the Israelites took the city of Jericho?

4. How do we know that the miracle of crossing the Jordan was not merely a matter of wading through shallow water in the time of drought? (Chaps. 3; 4)

5. What was the meaning of the twelve stones mentioned in Chapter 4?

6. When did the manna cease? (Chap. 5)

7. What was the Lord's strategy for taking Jericho? (6:1-5)

8. What became of Rahab and her family? (6:22-25)

9. What was Achan's sin? (7:1, 16-23)

10. How was the whole nation punished because of Achan's disobedience? (Chap. 7)

11. What strategy was used to take the city of Ai? (Chap. 8)

12. What evidence is there that all the company of Israel became familiar with the law of God? (8:32-35)

13. How did the Gibeonites deceive Joshua and to what work were they assigned? (Chap. 9)

14. What was the conflict into which Israel was drawn because of its treaty with Gibeon? (10:1-11)

15. In what supernatural way did the Lord aid Israel in the battle at Gibeon? (10:12-14)

16. Which two peoples or tribes of the land made peace with Israel? (Chap. 11)

17. How many kings did Joshua and the Israelites conquer? (Chap. 12)

*Program Leader*

A great deal of grace is required when a person is called on to do what Joshua did. Moses is thought by many to have been the greatest man in the Old Testament. Anyone who followed him would be almost certain to suffer by comparison. There is no evidence whatsoever that Joshua resented this situation. Rather, he dedicated all his powers and abilities to serving the Lord, and the Lord blessed his service.

(Closing Prayer)

# 13. The Division of the Promised Land

Scripture: Joshua 24:1-24

Suggested Hymns:

"O Worship the King"
"Who Is On the Lord's Side"
"Lead On, O King Eternal"

*Note to Program Leader*
(This is the second of two Bible study programs using the Book of Joshua. Ask the young people to read Chapters 13-24 before coming to the meeting and also to bring their Bibles to the program. Write the questions and references where all can see, distribute paper and pencils, and have the young people answer the questions from their Bibles. When all have finished their study, take up the questions one by one and compare answers. Allow time for discussion wherever it is desired or appropriate.)

*Program Leader's Introduction*
Joshua was not only a great military leader, which he obviously proved in directing the conquest of the land of Canaan, but he was an able administrator. He demonstrated this added ability when he led the people so wisely in the division of the land among the tribes. With twelve tribes to be satisfied in the distribution of territory, it was only natural that disagreements and disputes should arise. Joshua managed this difficult situation with relative ease, not only because he was a wise man, but because he was fully committed to doing the will of God. He is established not only as a great military leader, but as a great spiritual leader. So often the great men of the Bible made good beginnings and poor conclusions. Joshua was consistently spiritual from beginning to end.

## Questions for Study

1. Which tribe received no territory for an inheritance? (Chap. 13)

2. Which son of Jacob was father of two tribes? (Chap. 14)
3. How was the courage of Caleb demonstrated in his youth and in his old age? (14:6-15)
4. How well did Caleb succeed in wresting his inheritance from the hostile inhabitants? (15:13-19)
5. Who was the man who had no sons but whose daughters received an inheritance? (Chap. 17)
6. What was the advice of Joshua to the children of Joseph when they complained about their inheritance? (17:14-18) Contrast their attitude with Caleb's.
7. At the time when Israel gathered at Shiloh how many tribes had not yet received their inheritance? (Chap. 18)
8. Which tribe had its inheritance within the territory of another tribe? (Chap. 19)
9. What was the purpose of the "cities of refuge," and how many were there of them? (Chap. 20)
10. How many cities in all were given to the Levites? (Chap. 21)
11. What was the purpose of the altar built by the Reubenites and the Gadites? (Chap. 22)
12. Did Joshua claim personal credit for the victories over Israel's enemies? To whom did he give credit? (Chap. 23)
13. What was Joshua's advice to the people concerning worship and the word of God? (Chap. 23)
14. What stand did Joshua take in 24:15? Did the people follow his leading?
15. Would you say that the statement in 24:31 is a tribute to Joshua? In what way?

*Program Leader*

Any time an individual is able to exert such an influence on people that they continue to walk in his ways after he is gone, it is a high tribute. Joshua's loyalty to God made a lasting impression on the Israelites so that they in turn were loyal to the Lord for a generation after Joshua's death. This was an honor for him and it is a challenge to us.

(Closing Prayer)

# 14. Israel under Judges

Scripture: Judges 10:6-16

Suggested Hymns:

> "He Leadeth Me"
> "In the Hour of Trial"
> "O Love That Wilt Not Let Me Go"

*Suggestions to Program Leader*

(For the sake of variety, you may want to conduct this program as a contest. Divide the young people into two teams, see that each person has a Bible, read the questions distinctly giving the reference, and then award a point to the team which supplies the correct answer first. This will mean that you, as the leader, should have already located the answers and written them down before the meeting begins. Do not rush through the questions, but allow time for discussion after each one.)

*Program Leader's Introduction*

This is the first of two programs in which we shall study the Book of Judges. The period of history covered in this book extends from the entry of Israel into the land of promise until the time of Samuel, who is generally considered to be the last of the Judges. It was a period of roughly two centuries.

A rapid reading of the book of Judges reveals that these were times of disorganization, lawlessness, and violence. It is sometimes said that Judges is a book of cycles. By this it is meant that the same general course of events was repeated time after time. The Israelites would forsake God's laws and worship and fall into idolatry. Then God would allow some of the pagan nations to conquer and oppress them. After a time of oppression the Israelites would repent, and then God would raise up a judge to deliver them from their enemies. In time they would forsake the Lord again, and the cycle would be repeated.

It may seem that human history goes around in circles without making any progress, but we know that God's hand is in it all, and He is always moving toward His righteous goal. In our study of this book we shall see the repeated faithlessness of God's people, but we can also see the patience and the purpose of God.

## Questions for Study and Discussion

1. What did the angel say would be the result of Israel's compromise with the pagan peoples of the land? (2:1-3)
2. According to 2:16-19 what was the cycle that was repeated again and again during this period?
3. What is the special tribute paid to Joshua in 2:7?
4. What were the practices of the Israelites which led so often to compromise? (3:5-7)
5. Who was the first judge? (Chap. 3)
6. After he had slain Eglon, what clever measures did Ehud take to insure his escape? (3:14-26)
7. Who was the woman who judged Israel and who was her general? (4:3-9)
8. Who was the woman who delivered Sisera to Barak and how did she do it? (4:15-22)
9. Why did Gideon think he was justified in questioning God's promise to be with Israel and help them? (6:13)
10. What sign did the angel give of God's power and presence? (6:17-21)
11. What did Gideon do to demonstrate his faith and leadership? (6:25-27)
12. Why were the people afraid because of what Gideon had done, and what was his father's answer to them? (6:28-32)
13. What request did Gideon make of God? (6:36-40)
14. Why did the Lord want Gideon's army reduced in size? (7:2)
15. How did Gideon learn that the Midianites respected God's power? (7:9-14)
16. How did the Lord bring about the conquest of the Midianites? (7:19-22)
17. How does Gideon's statement in 8:23 show his spirituality?
18. How was Abimelech's evil punished? (9:52-56)
19. What did the Lord say to the unfaithful Israelites, and what was their response? (10:10-16)

*Program Leader*

There may come times in our own lives which will remind us

of the era of the judges. It may seem that we are "going around in circles" and that no real progress is being made in our lives. These are times when we need to rededicate ourselves to the Lord, remembering that He is God and that His righteous purposes will be fulfilled.

(Closing Prayer)

# 15. Israel under Judges (concluded)

Scriptures: Judges 16:21-30

Suggested Hymns:

> "Jesus Calls Us: O'er the Tumult"
> "I Need Thee Every Hour"
> "O Master, Let Me Walk with Thee"

*Suggestions for Program Leader*

(Provide the young people with Bibles, paper, and pencils. Give them the study questions with the references provided. It would be best to give each person a copy of the questions. If you cannot do this, copy the questions on a chalk board or on a large piece of paper or cardboard so that all can see. If neither of these procedures is possible, you can read the questions distinctly, repeating when necessary. When the young people have completed their answers, go over the questions aloud comparing and discussing answers. The leader should have answered all the questions first. If you have any difficulty, ask your minister or adult advisor. If possible, it is desirable to have the minister present for the discussion period.)

*Program Leader's Introduction*

We noticed in the last program that the time of the judges was a period of disorganization, lawlessness, and violence. These characteristics seem to be even more prominent in that last half of the book, which we shall be studying in this program. We need to remind ourselves once more that even when men seem to forget God, God does not forget them nor does He forsake His own plan and purpose in the world. We can see the hand of God at work in the lives and times of the judges.

One of the characteristics of the Bible which is especially prominent in this part of the book of Judges is its honesty. Most books, even history books, are slanted in favor of certain persons or certain points of view. It ought to impress us that the Bible makes no attempt to cover up or apologize for the failures of its human heroes. God chose Samson and used him as one of the outstanding judges of this period, but the Bible does not try to gloss over Samson's grievous sins and weaknesses. There is no attempt to hide his failures. A book which is so obviously honest in the way it presents its chief characters certainly commends itself to our faith and trust.

As we study these last chapters of the Book of Judges, let us remember that God did not approve of many things that these people did, but let us notice how He ruled and overruled in their lives so that His work was accomplished.

## Questions for Study

1. What was Jephthah's foolish vow, and what was its tragic result? (11:29-40)
2. What test did the Gileadites use to identify the Ephramites? (12:5-6)
3. Who were the three men who judged Israel after Jephthah? (12:7-15)
4. What was a Nazarite? (13:5-7)
5. How did the angel prove his divine appointment to Manoah and his wife? (13:16-21)
6. What did Samson's father and mother think of his choice of a wife? (14:3)
7. What is the meaning of Samson's statement: "If ye had not plowed with my heifer, ye had not found out my riddle"?
8. What evidences are there that God overruled the events growing out of Samson's poor choice of a wife? (14:4, 19)
9. What destructive stunt did Samson perform after he had learned that his wife had been given to another man? (15:3-5)
10. What became of Samson's wife and her family as a result of this incident? (15:6)
11. What do you think of the decision of the men of Judah to bind Samson themselves and to deliver him to the Philistines?
12. What happened when the men of Gaza tried to trap Samson in their city? (16:1-3)
13. What was Delilah promised by the Philistines if she would betray Samson? (16:5)

14. What were the three wrong answers Samson gave to Delilah? (16:6-14)
15. What was the real reason for Samson's weakness? (16:20)
16. What evidence is there that Samson finally remembered his need of God's presence and power? (16:28)
17. Do you think Samson was a Nazarite at heart as well as outwardly?
18. How did Samson misuse his abilities? What are the abilities and opportunities we have today which we may be tempted to misuse in a similar way?
19. How do the "image" and the "hired priest" in Chapter 17 indicate the spiritual depths to which Israel had sunk?
20. How does 21:25 sum up the lawlessness and the godlessness of the times of the judges?

*Program Leader*

It is discouraging to see people who have a rich spiritual heritage depart from it and live like pagans. This is what happened in the times of the judges. At different times and in different places it has continued to happen ever since. If and when we see such a departure taking place around us, it is time to renew our own faith in the righteousness and power of God.

(Closing Prayer)

# 16. Ruth

Scripture: Ruth 1:8-17

Suggested Hymns:

"O God, the Rock of Ages"
"God Moves in a Mysterious Way"
"My Faith Looks Up to Thee"

## Program Leader's Introduction

The Book of Ruth deals with the same period of history as the Book of Judges, but the temper of the two books is not the same. Judges tells largely of strife, violence, and degeneracy. Ruth is an account of beauty and love and faith. It is hard to realize that a man like Boaz lived in the period of the judges, but he did. The fact that he did proves the point that however wicked men become and however degenerate the times, God does not leave Himself without a faithful witness. It also proves that, as the Lord's people, we do not have to yield to temptations or allow our lives to be conformed to the world of wickedness around us.

(Now allow time for the young people to read silently the four chapters of the Book of Ruth. When all have finished reading, ask the discussion questions, allowing time after each for full discussion. Ask your minister or some other Bible authority to be present to answer difficult questions which may arise.)

## Questions for Study and Discussion

1. Why did Elimelech and his family go to Moab? Why was their decision spiritually dangerous?
2. Why did Naomi decide to return to her native land after the death of her sons?
3. What opinion did Naomi seem to have of her daughters-in-law?
4. Why did Naomi insist that Orpah and Ruth remain in Moab? Why would it have been easier for them to find husbands in Moab than in Israel?

5. In what sense was Ruth's decision to accompany Naomi a spiritual one?

6. What are the indications that Naomi was bitter? (1:13, 20-21).

7. Was it really by accident (2:3) that Ruth gleaned in the fields of Boaz? How do you explain this development?

8. What is indicated about the character of Boaz by his greeting to his workers and by their response?

9. Why might Boaz's servants have treated Ruth roughly?

10. What provisions did Boaz make for Ruth's safety and comfort and for her success as a gleaner?

11. Since gleaning was a very temporary way of earning a living, what provisions did Naomi seek to make for the future?

12. What proof have we that Boaz was an honorable man, and what are the indications that he loved and respected Ruth?

13. Why was the man who was nearer kin than Boaz unwilling to assume the obligation of the near kinsman?

14. How is it indicated that Naomi recovered from her bitterness?

15. Who was Ruth's most famous descendant? (Be careful how you answer this one.)

*Program Leader*

In our study of the Old Testament we often tend to think that God's blessings were only for the literal Israelites, those alone who were the actual physical descendants of Jacob. The story of Ruth proves that God honors and rewards true faith wherever it is found.

(Closing Prayer)

# 17. The Childhood and Early Ministry of Samuel

Scripture: I Samuel 3:1-10

Suggested Hymns:

"Where He Leads Me I Will Follow"
"Who Is On the Lord's Side?"
"Lead On, O King Eternal"

*Suggestions to Program Leader*

(Have the young people read the first ten chapters of I Samuel before coming to the meeting. If this cannot be done, use the first part of the program time for reading these ten chapters. Distribute paper and pencils, and ask the young people, with Bibles closed, to write out the answers to the questions below. When all have finished, let each check his own paper as you read out the correct answers from the Bible. This will mean that you must have located and marked the answers beforehand.)

### Questions

1. Who was Hannah's husband?
2. How many wives did he have?
3. Why was Hannah bitter?
4. What did Eli think when he saw Hannah praying silently in the temple?
5. What did Eli promise Hannah would happen?
6. What did Hannah do with Samuel after she had weaned him?
7. How did Eli's sons show their greed?
8. What were the names of Eli's sons?
9. What did Samuel think when he heard the voice calling his name in the night?
10. What message did God give Samuel concerning Eli?
11. What did all Israel believe would be young Samuel's future work?

12. What happened to Eli when he heard that the ark of the covenant was captured?
13. Why did Eli's daughter-in-law name her child Ichabod?
14. What happened to the god Dagon when the Philistines brought the ark of God into Ashdod?
15. How did the Philistines send the ark back to the Israelites?
16. What befell the Philistines at Mizpeh?
17. Where was Samuel's house?
18. How were Samuel's sons like Eli's?
19. What did the people desire of Samuel instead of a judge like himself?
20. Why did the people say they wanted a king?
21. To which one of the tribes of Israel did Saul belong?
22. Why did Saul seek Samuel's help?
23. What did Saul do when he was in the company of the prophets and the Spirit of God came upon him?
24. Who did Samuel say the people had really rejected as their ruler?
25. What does the Bible say about Saul's physical height?

### Questions for Discussion

(To be considered after the answers to the papers are checked.)
1. What does the situation in Elkanah's household reveal about plural marriage even among otherwise good people?
2. Why did it require courage for Samuel to tell Eli about the vision from God?
3. How did the character of Samuel's sons contribute to Israel's desire for a king?
4. How is the "herd instinct" illustrated in Israel's desire for a king?
5. In what sense did the people reject God when they insisted on having a king?

### Program Leader

Samuel was one of the ablest and most dedicated leaders Israel ever had. Surely it must have been discouraging when the people of the nation insisted upon having a king. Their insistence upon being ruled over by a king meant that they were, in effect, rejecting Samuel. Samuel might well have washed his hands of them, but he did not. He was dedicated to God and was much more concerned that the people had rejected God's plan for the nation than he was that they had rejected him personally. This proves the bigness of the man.

(Closing Prayer)

# 18. Saul's Downfall and David's Rise

Scripture: I Samuel 13:5-14

Suggested Hymns:

> "Trust and Obey"
> "He Leadeth Me, O Blessed Thought"
> "Have Thine Own Way, Lord"

*Suggestions to Program Leader*

(This is another program of Bible study. The passage to be used is I Samuel 11-20. Ask the young people to read these ten chapters before coming to the meeting. If you have as many as nine young people, you may divide them into three groups assigning them the following chapters and questions: Group 1—Chapters 11-14 and Questions 1-8; Group 2—Chapters 15-17 and Questions 9-17; and Group 3—Chapters 18-20 and Questions 18-25. Let each small group find the answers to their questions using their Bibles. Then reassemble and let each small group report, reading both questions and answers. If it is not practical to divide into small groups, let all the young people together study the whole passage looking up the answers to all the questions. When you have studied the passage by using the study questions, allow time for discussion. Four starter discussion questions are suggested at the end of the printed program material.)

*Study Questions*

1. What unusual method did Saul use when he sent the message to summon the army of Israel?
2. Did Samuel think he had been a just judge? How do you know?
3. According to Samuel, who had been king of Israel prior to Saul's kingship?
4. In answer to Samuel's request, what sign did God give which proved that the people were wicked?

5. What happened (Chap. 13) to arouse the enmity of the Philistines to such a point that the Israelites were greatly afraid of them?

6. What did Saul do in preparation for the battle with the Philistines that was displeasing to God?

7. What action did the people take when Saul was about to punish Jonathan because he had violated his father's ruling and broken the fast?

8. How does 14:52 fulfill Samuel's prediction in 8:11-12?

9. How did Saul disobey the Lord in the matter of the Amalekites?

10. Did Saul tell the whole truth (15:13)? Explain.

11. What did Samuel mean when he said, "To obey is better than sacrifice, and to hearken than the fat of rams"?

12. What did Samuel say would be the result of Saul's disobedience?

13. What did Samuel do to Agag?

14. What is the difference between man's judgment and God's? (16:7)

15. How many of Jesse's sons were in Saul's army when he sent David to inquire about them?

16. What was it about Goliath that especially angered David?

17. Why was David sure he would be victorious over Goliath?

18. What did Jonathan give to David as a sign of their friendship?

19. Why did Saul become jealous of David?

20. Why was Saul willing for his daughter to become David's wife?

21. What success did Jonathan have in his first attempt to intercede with Saul on behalf of David?

22. How did Michal save David from Saul's scheme to kill him?

23. What happened to Saul's messengers when they came to Ramah?

24. What signal did Jonathan and David arrange to indicate Saul's attitude toward David?

25. What was Saul's attitude toward Jonathan when he tried to defend David at the meal?

## Questions for Discussion

1. What evidence is there that Saul refused to accept the responsibility for his own sin and the downfall that was consequent to it?
2. What are some of the areas in which we may be tempted to run ahead of God (making our own decisions without seeking His will)?
3. What might be some modern applications of the truth: "To obey is better than sacrifice, and to hearken than the fat of rams"?
4. What is the warning and the comfort in the last part of 16:7?

*Program Leader*

Saul's pride and jealousy resulted in his downfall. It is sad to see, or even read of, such an experience. Saul began his reign trusting in the Lord. He ended it seeking the advice of a witch. It is not surprising that he lost the favor and blessing of God. In the meanwhile, God had brought another man on the scene, David the son of Jesse, a young man of humility, faith, and great ability. As long as a throne remained in Jerusalem it was called the "throne of David." This fact indicates the great love that both God and the people had for David.

(Closing Prayer)

# 19. The Final Failure of Saul

Scripture: I Samuel 26:1-21

Suggested Hymns:

> "In the Hour of Trial"
> "Take Time to Be Holy"
> "My Faith Looks Up to Thee"

*Suggestions to Program Leader*

(This is our third Bible study program based on I Samuel. Again we are using study questions, but are suggesting that they be used in a slightly different way. Ask the young people to read chapters 21-31 of I Samuel before coming to the meeting. After the devotional service, read the study questions one at a time. Ask your young people to give the correct answers including the place in the Bible where the answer is found. Let the first one who knows or can find the answer give it. Open Bibles may be used, of course. After you have completed answering the study questions, take up the "Thought and Discussion Questions," allowing ample time for discussion of each.)

## Study Questions

1. Whose sword did the priest give to David?
2. Why did David pretend madness?
3. What kind of people associated themselves with David at the cave of Adullam?
4. Who told Saul how Ahimelech had helped David?
5. What cruel thing did Doeg do at Saul's command?
6. Why was Saul not successful in finding and harming David?
7. What people sought to deliver David to Saul?
8. How did David prove (chap. 24) that he had no desire to harm Saul?
9. How did Saul react to David's kindness?
10. What promise did David make to Saul?
11. Where was Samuel buried?
12. How did Nabal answer David's servants?

13. Who persuaded David not to destroy Nabal?
14. How did David prove (chap. 26) that he still intended no harm to Saul?
15. Of what carelessness did David accuse Abner?
16. What did Saul promise to David and what admission did he make?
17. What was the name of the place which Achish gave to David?
18. Why did Saul need the help of the witch of Endor?
19. Why was the witch afraid?
20. What did the woman urge Saul to do afer he had conversed with Samuel?
21. Why did the princes of the Philistines not trust David?
22. Who gave David information that led to his victory over the Amalekites?
23. To whom did David give the spoil of the Amalekites?
24. Where were Saul and his sons slain?
25. What did Saul's armor bearer refuse to do?

## Thought and Discussion Questions

1. Why did David refuse to harm Saul when he had opportunities to do so and Saul was seeking at the very time to kill him?
2. Do you think Saul's words "I have played the fool and have erred exceedingly" could be descriptive of his whole reign? Why?
3. Why was David thankful for Abigail's advice and intervention?
4. Why was it that a time came when Saul could no longer receive wisdom and guidance from the Lord? What meaning does this have for us today?
5. What special wisdom did David show in 30:26? How would this act be helpful to him in future years?

## Program Leader

One adjustment in Saul's attitude could well have changed the whole course of his life. If, in the early years of his reign, he had consistently and patiently sought the will of the Lord, things would have been much different toward the end of his reign. Many are the times when we are tempted to be impatient—to go ahead with what seems right to us without asking God to make known to us what is His will. When such temptations come, let us remember Saul and the terrible tragedy that came to him.

(Closing Prayer)

# 20. The Establishment of the Throne of David

Scripture: II Samuel 3:1, 17-21

Suggested Hymns:

"Saviour, Like a Shepherd Lead Us"
"Come, Thou Fount of Every Blessing"
"O for a Heart to Praise My God"

*Suggestions to Program Leader*
(If possible, prepare a list of the study questions for each young person. If this is not possible, write them on the chalk board or on a large piece of paper. Ask the young people, using their Bibles for Chapters 1-12, to write out the answers to the questions. When all have finished, let each check his answers as you read out the correct answers which you will have prepared beforehand. Then proceed to the discussion questions. Allow time for the full discussion of each question and for any additional questions that may be raised. If you do not get immediate volunteers for the discussion period, you may need to call on some individuals for their ideas.)

*Study Questions*

1. Was the Amalekite telling the truth when he said that he had killed Saul? Why do you think he made the claim that he did?
2. How long did David reign in Hebron?
3. Who did Abner make king over Israel?
4. Who was Asahel?
5. How does 3:1 summarize the struggle between the house of David and the house of Saul?
6. Why did Abner become angry with Ishbosheth?
7. Why was Joab so anxious to kill Abner?
8. Who killed Ishbosheth?
9. How did David reward the men who killed Ishbosheth?
10. How old was David when he began to reign over all Israel?

11. To whom did David give credit for his victory over the Philistines?
12. What befell Uzzah?
13. How did David react to the death of Uzzah?
14. What was the message of the Lord to David concerning the building of the temple?
15. What did David do with the silver and gold which he had taken from conquered nations?
16. What was Joab's official position in the kingdom of David?
17. What did David do for Mephibosheth and why?
18. How did Mephibosheth become lame?
19. What did Hanum suspect concerning David's ambassadors?
20. What strategy did Joab and Abishai use against the Ammonites?
21. What sin might David have avoided if he had gone with his armies rather than remaining in Jerusalem?
22. Who was really responsible for Uriah's death, and how did he arrange it?
23. What was the point of the story Nathan told David?
24. How did David indicate his belief in life after death?

*Discussion Questions*

1. Do you think David was ordinarily generous toward his enemies? In which incidents are his attitudes indicated?
2. How did David show that he trusted God for guidance and gave Him credit for victories and prosperity?
3. What do you think contributed to David's moral and spiritual lapse?
4. What can we learn from the way David responded to Nathan's (God's) judgment of his sin?

*Program Leader*

One of the refreshing qualities of the Bible is its frank and honest treatment of its heroes. David is certainly one of the great heroes of Scripture, but no attempt is made to excuse or gloss over his weakness and sin. Perhaps one of the marks of his greatness was his ready willingness to confess his sin and to accept responsibility for his own wrongdoing. In this record of God's dealings with David, we see very clearly that, although the Lord will not excuse our sinfulness, He is ever ready to forgive us when we come to Him with honest confession and faith.

(Closing Prayer)

# 21. Trouble for the Throne of David

Scripture: II Samuel 22:1-18

Suggested Hymns:

"A Wonderful Saviour Is Jesus My Lord"
"I Would Be True"
"Blessed Assurance"

*Suggestions to Program Leader*
(This program will be based on II Samuel 13-24. If possible, have the young people read these twelve chapters before coming to the meeting. Divide the group into teams and let them sit facing each other. Read out the study questions one at a time, and let the young people supply the answers from their Bibles or from memory, if they can. Award a point to the team which can give the correct answer first. You, as the program leader, will need to have looked up and written out the correct answers before coming to the meeting. When the quiz has been completed, take up the discussion questions and talk about them fully.)

## Study Questions

1. What did Absalom have done to Ammon?
2. What was the point of the story told by the woman of Tekoah to David?
3. What very unusual physical characteristic did Absalom have?
4. What drastic measure did Absalom use to attract Joab's attention?
5. How did Absalom win the affection of the people of Israel?
6. Where did Absalom establish himself as king?
7. How did Mephibosheth show his treachery and lack of appreciation to David?
8. What did Shimei do to David?
9. How did the woman of Bahurim hide the messengers?
10. What did Ahithophel do when he saw that his advice was not taken?

11. What command did David give his generals concerning the treatment of Absalom?
12. Who killed Absalom?
13. How did Cushi announce the death of Absalom to David?
14. Why did Joab criticize David when he mourned for Absalom?
15. What treatment of Shimei did Abishai urge?
16. What was the name of the Benjamite who led a rebellion against David?
17. Who killed Amasa?
18. Who promised Joab the head of Sheba?
19. What did the Gibeonites request of David by way of restitution for Saul's cruelty to them?
20. What was the name of the giant whom Abishai killed?
21. What was the occasion of David's song of praise to the Lord?
22. Why did David refuse to drink water brought to him by his warriors at such great danger to themselves?
23. What were the three choices of punishment David had?
24. In what touching way did David intercede for the people and offer to take their punishment on himself?
25. Why did David insist on paying for Araunah's threshing floor?

## Discussion Questions

1. Do you think many of David's problems can be traced to his having many wives? Explain.
2. What do you think of Absalom's techniques for attaining popularity? Can you think of instances where similar methods are practiced today? Give examples.
3. What valuable principle concerning our service to the Lord is illustrated by David's decision to pay for Araunah's threshing floor?

### Program Leader

The Bible says, "Let him that thinketh he standeth take heed lest he fall." It is certain that David was well established spiritually when he came to the throne of Israel. He stood on firm spiritual ground. It is quite possible, however, that a time came when he was complacent about his spiritual condition. Indeed, this seems to have been the case. It was at this time that his trouble began to multiply. If we really know the Lord and are close to Him, let us give thanks, but let us also remember how important it is that we renew our dedication every day.

(Closing Prayer)

# 22. Solomon's Reign

Scripture: I Kings 9:1-9

Suggested Hymns:

"Lead On, O King Eternal"
"All to Jesus I Surrender"
"My Jesus, I Love Thee"

*Suggestions to Program Leader*
(Request the young people to read carefully Chapters 1-11 of I Kings before coming to the program. For the fun of friendly competition, divide them into two teams. Then, with Bibles open, read the questions printed below one by one. Award one point to the team whose member stands first with the correct answer to each question. You, as leader, will need to have located the answers beforehand. You may ask an adult, perhaps your minister, to be judge. When the contest is completed and the winning team has been congratulated, take up the discussion questions. Address these to the whole group and invite their response.)

*Program Leader's Introduction*
From the standpoint of wealth, fame, power, and military might, Solomon's reign was the high point in Israel's history. If a sensitive, spiritual observer had been on the scene, however, he would surely have seen obvious signs of moral and spiritual decline. For one thing, there was the King's obsession with material wealth. His buildings, especially his own home, were lavishly and extravagantly appointed. Emphasis seemed to be on these things rather than on things of the spirit. Then too, there were Solomon's wives. The Bible says he "loved many strange women." So great was their number that "many" is hardly the word for it. It is not likely that he really loved all these women. Some of them were surely married for political advantage. But, even so, these women had their effect on Solomon, and it was not good. They induced him to compromise in

the matter of worshipping God only. It was God who made Solomon and his kingdom great. When he forsook God, his kingdom began to decline.

We shall now have some questions on the first eleven chapters of I Kings, and as we find the answers to these questions we shall learn more of the story of Solomon.

## Study Questions

1. What did Adonijah do that reminds us of his brother, Absalom?
2. Who first intervened with David on behalf of Solomon, and who suggested this course of action?
3. What did Adonijah do when he learned that Solomon had been proclaimed king by David's order?
4. What sound advice did David give Solomon before he died?
5. What was the condition under which Shimei would be allowed to live in safety?
6. What did Solomon ask of the Lord, and what did he receive?
7. How was Solomon's wisdom demonstrated in his decision concerning the two women who were disputing over the living child?
8. How many proverbs and songs are attributed to Solomon?
9. What postponed project did Solomon tell Hiram he intended to undertake?
10. What were the commodities exchanged between Solomon and Hiram?
11. In which year did Solomon begin to build the temple?
12. What conditions was Solomon to fulfill in order for the Lord to "perform" His word to Solomon as He had to David?
13. Which took longer, the building of Solomon's house or the building of the house of the Lord?
14. Of what material were the temple vessels made?
15. Where in the temple was the ark of the covenant placed?
16. Why were the priests unable to do their work in the temple when it was first being dedicated?
17. How many days were the people engaged in dedicating the temple?
18. How did the Lord respond to Solomon's prayer of dedication?

19. Who instructed Solomon's servants in seamanship?
20. Why did the Queen of Sheba come to visit Solomon, and what was her appraisal of him?
21. What was Solomon's chief sin, and who led him to it?
22. How did the Lord say He would punish Solomon for his unfaithfulness?
23. What was the meaning of Ahijah's act when he tore the garment in pieces?
24. Why did Solomon seek to kill Jeroboam?

### Questions for Discussion

1. According to the descriptions given in the Bible, which do you think was more elaborate, the house of the Lord or the house of Solomon?
2. What do you think of David's instructions to Solomon regarding his (David's) enemies?
3. When Solomon worshipped the gods of his pagan wives, do you suppose he ceased worshipping the Lord altogether? Even if he did not, is the Lord satisfied with a divided loyalty?

### Program Leader

It has well been said that "God has no grandchildren." Each person must become personally related to God. We receive many benefits and blessings because of the strong faith of our parents, but their closeness to the Lord does not guarantee ours. Solomon was blessed because of the spirituality of David, but this did not make it unnecessary for Solomon to live close to the Lord himself.

(Closing Prayer)

# 23. God's People Divided

Scripture: I Kings 12:1-11

Suggested Hymns:

> "O Worship the King"
> "I Would Be True"
> "All the Way My Saviour Leads Me"

*Suggestions to Program Leader*

(In order to be better prepared for this Bible study program, ask the young people to read I Kings 12-22 before coming to the meeting. If possible, have enough copies of the study questions for each young person. If this is not feasible, write the questions on the chalkboard—you may have to write a few questions at a time, then erase them and write more. Distribute pencils and paper, and ask the young people to write out brief answers to the questions after they have looked them up in their Bibles. When all have completed their answers, go over the questions together, comparing answers.)

*Program Leader's Introduction*

In this portion of the Bible we come to an era of Israel's history which is not very encouraging. It is obviously a period of moral and spiritual decline. The times were characterized by folly and faithlessness, violence and treachery. While some of the rulers had long and relatively peaceful reigns, it seems that being king was a very insecure job most of the time. No sooner would a man establish himself on the throne by force when someone else would begin to plot against him with a view to slaying him and all his family. This situation was characteristic of both Judah and Israel, but it was especially true of the northern kingdom where faithlessness and rebellion against God's truth were more pronounced.

As we search the last eleven chapters of I Kings for the answers to our study questions we will understand how displeased God must have been with most of His people during those

70

years. On the other hand, we shall see that all through these sinful times God was preserving a faithful witness to Himself. This should be of great encouragement to us in those times when we feel that all is against us and that there is no appreciation of righteousness.

## Study Questions

1. Which were the two groups of people that advised Rehoboam?
2. What advice did each group give, and which did Rehoboam accept?
3. Which two tribes remained loyal to Rehoboam?
4. What did Jeroboam give as his reason for building places of worship in Dan and Bethel?
5. What kind of people did Jeroboam choose to be priests?
6. What happened to Jeroboam when he tried to lay hands on a prophet?
7. How did the old prophet try to mislead the man of God, and what was the final result?
8. Why did Jeroboam send his wife to the prophet Ahijah, and what did Ahijah tell her?
9. What did Rehoboam use to replace the golden shields which the Egyptians carried away?
10. How long did Rehoboam reign?
11. Who was the king who removed his mother from being queen, and why did he do it?
12. How did Omri compare with the kings who had gone before him and with the one who immediately followed him?
13. How was Elijah fed while he lived by the brook Cherith?
14. What happened to the meal and the oil of the widow who fed Elijah?
15. What notable miracle was performed in the woman's house (besides sustaining the food)?
16. How had Obadiah, the servant of Ahab, proved his respect for God at great danger to himself?
17. Of what did Ahab accuse Elijah, and how did Elijah turn the accusation back on Ahab?
18. How did Elijah propose to test the prophets of Baal, and what was the result of the test?

19. What was Elijah's attitude when he slept under the juniper tree, and how did God answer him?
20. What did the prophet say to Ahab about his having spared Benhadad, king of Syria?
21. How did Jezebel arrange to have Naboth's vineyard given to Ahab?
22. What did Elijah prophesy concerning the end of Ahab and Jezebel?
23. What makes it appear that Jehoshaphat did not trust Ahab's prophets?
24. What did Micaiah prophesy about the campaign against Syria?
25. How did Ahab try to avoid detection during the battle, and what happened to him?

*Program Leader*

While we are never justified in condoning evil, it is surely comforting to know that God so rules and overrules in the affairs of men that His righteous purposes are carried out.

(Closing Prayer)

# 24. A Successor for Elijah

Scripture: II Kings 2:1-15

Suggested Hymns:

"Lord, Speak to Me That I May Speak"
"A Charge to Keep I Have"
"Wonderful Words of Life"

*Suggestions to Program Leader*
(To present this program choose a panel of three or four persons. Ask them to make a careful study of II Kings 1-8 before meeting time, using the study questions below. For the program, arrange the panel members around a table, and address the study questions to them in turn. After the one questioned has made his answer, allow the other panel members to make their comments and observations. Be sure it is understood that those on the panel and the other young people will use their Bibles during the study and discussion.)

*Program Leader's Introduction*
Many rulers of both Judah and Israel are mentioned in the first eight chapters of II Kings, but the most prominent personality is Elisha, the prophet, the successor to Elijah. Surely as we read these chapters many of the words and actions of Elisha seem harsh to our minds and ears. We must bear in mind, though, the characteristics of the times—the superstitions, rebelliousness, and wickedness of the people. Stern measures were required to make them mindful of God and of their obligations to Him. God repeatedly revealed Himself to these people in judgment and in mighty power. Even so, the impression made on them was not very lasting. We are amazed that they could have been so callous until we remember how we are so often ungrateful for God's blessings and so unconcerned about His promised judgment. As we study these chapters together, let us think about ourselves and our relation to the Lord as well as about those people of long ago.

*Questions for Study and Discussion*

1. What was Elijah's message to Ahaziah?
2. How many times and by whom did Ahaziah send for Elijah? Why do you think Elijah dealt so harshly with these messengers?
3. For what did Elisha ask before Elijah was taken away? Do you think he made a wise request?
4. What was the first evidence that Elisha had received Elijah's spirit?
5. What helpful miracle was performed by Elisha for the people of Jericho?
6. In what way was Jehoram's reign an improvement over that of his father, Ahab?
7. For what reason only was Elisha willing to confer with Jehoram? What does this say about the relative character of the two nations?
8. What did the Moabites think when they saw the sun shining on the water in the valley, and what happened to them?
9. What did the king of Moab do with his eldest son?
10. What did Elisha do for the widow whose two sons were about to be taken into bondage?
11. What did the Shunammite woman do for Elisha, and why do you think she did it?
12. What was the first thing Elisha directed to be done when he learned that the Shunammite woman's son was dead?
13. What did Elisha do at Gilgal to counteract the poison in the people's food?
14. Why was the king of Israel upset when he read the king of Syria's letter? What does this reveal about his relation to God?
15. Why was Naaman offended at Elisha's prescribed treatment for his illness, and how is the wisdom of his servants shown?
16. What was Gehazi's sin and how was he punished?
17. Why were the workmen especially concerned when the axe fell into the water?
18. What did the man of God mean when he said: "Fear not: for they that be with us are more than they that be with them"?
19. What did Elisha mean when he said to the king's compan-

ion: "Thou shalt see it with thine eyes, but shalt not eat thereof"?

20. Why had the Syrians fled from Samaria?
21. How did the people of Samaria come to know that the Syrians had fled? What commendable spirit is seen among the lepers in this incident?
22. How did Benhadad die, and who killed him?
23. What did Elisha predict concerning Hazael, and what was Hazael's reaction to the prediction?
24. How does the Bible account for Ahaziah's being so evil?

*Program Leader*

Naaman, the Syrian general, was offended when Elisha said that he should prove his faith in God by dipping himself seven times in the river Jordan. Naaman expected that something more impressive would be done or required due to the seriousness of his illness and the importance of his person. Simple faith in God was all that was needed. We too are often inclined to have our own ideas about how God should bless us and meet our needs. We need to bear in mind that the one essential thing is to trust the Lord implicitly. If we do, we shall find that His grace is sufficient and His way is best.

(Closing Prayer)

# 25. The Decline and Fall of the Kingdom of Israel

Scripture: II Kings 17:7-19

Suggested Hymns:

"Trust and Obey"
"Living for Jesus"
"Only Trust Him"

*Suggestions to Program Leader*

(To make preparation for this program, ask the young people to read Chapters 9-17 of II Kings before coming to the meeting. If time permits, you may let them read over these chapters very briefly at the beginning of the program. Provide paper and pencils and have them answer the thirty "yes and no" questions with their Bibles closed. Then, open the Bibles and let each person check his own answers with the aid of the references supplied at the end of each question. To heighten interest, you may divide the young people into two teams and average the score of each team to see which was best informed. When this part of the program is completed, address the discussion questions to the whole group and allow ample time after each question for discussion and comment.)

*Program Leader's Introduction*

The period of history described in II Kings 9-17 must have been discouraging to any person living at that time who really loved the Lord. The Southern Kingdom of Judah had its "ups" and "downs." There were good kings and bad kings—times of revival and times of spiritual relapse. Year by year the nation grew weaker from an economic and military standpoint. Even though there were times of spiritual improvement, Judah never reached the material or spiritual heights the nation had known during the reign of David.

Israel, the Northern Kingdom, was even more discouraging.

The only bright place in Israel's history was temporary material progress from time to time. Morally and spiritually speaking, there were no "ups" and "downs" in Israel—only a steady decline. Each king and each generation of people seemed determined to be more idolatrous and less loyal to the Lord than those who had gone before. Increasingly, the characteristics of the nation were these: idolatry, immorality, violence, treachery, and injustice. If Assyria had not taken Israel, the nation would surely have destroyed itself. In reality Israel did destroy itself— Assyria was merely the agent God used to chastise Israel because of her sin.

### Study Questions

1. Was Elisha himself the prophet who annointed Jehu to be king of Israel? (9:1-3)
2. Did the prophet who annointed Jehu predict that Jezebel would die a natural death and be buried? (9:10)
3. Did the watchman identify Jehu by his furious driving? (9:20)
4. Was it Jehu's armor bearer who killed King Jehoram? (9:24)
5. Was it the eunuchs who threw Jezebel to her death? (9:32-33)
6. Did Jehu spare any of the descendents of Ahab? (10:11, 17)
7. Was Jehu sincere when he announced that he would serve Baal more than Ahab did? (10:18-28)
8. Did Jehu forsake idolatry altogether? (10:29)
9. Was Athaliah completely successful in her attempt to destroy all King Ahaziah's descendents? (11:1-2)
10. Did the priest order that Athaliah should not be put to death in the temple? (11:13-16)
11. Did Jehoash, the son of Ahaziah, King of Judah, do what was right in God's sight? (12:2)
12. Did the people gather money to repair the temple by placing their offerings in a chest with a hole in the lid? (12:7-11)
13. When the Lord delivered Israel from the oppression of the Syrians during the reign of Jehu's son, did the people turn again to the Lord? (13:1-6)

14. Was Elisha displeased when Joash, King of Israel struck the ground only three times? (13:19)
15. Did the dead man who was buried in Elisha's grave revive? (13:21)
16. Was Amaziah, King of Judah, a good king? (14:1-3)
17. Was Jehoash, King of Israel, favorable to the idea of a meeting with Amaziah? (14:8-14)
18. Was the second King Jeroboam of Israel a God-fearing man? (14:24)
19. Was he (Jeroboam) successful in his military campaigns? (14:28)
20. Was King Azariah of Judah a leper? (15:5)
21. Was the promise fulfilled that Jehu's descendents to the fourth generation would sit on the throne of Israel? (15:12)
22. Did Menahem, King of Israel, pay tribute to the king of Assyria? (15:9)
23. Was Pekah Pekahiah's son? (15:25)
24. Was Pekah removed from the throne of Israel in much the same way that he had removed Pekahiah? (15:25, 30)
25. Did Ahaz, King of Judah, walk in the ways of David? (16:2)
26. Did Ahaz give the gold and silver out of the temple to the king of Assyria as well as the treasures of his own house? (16:8)
27. Did Ahaz pattern a new altar after one he had seen in Damasucus? (16:10-11)
28. Did Hoshea, King of Israel, try to secure the help of Egypt against the Assyrians? (17:4)
29. Wat it because of idolatry only that the Lord allowed Israel to be taken captive? (17:7-18)
30. Were the people of Judah fully pleasing to the Lord? (17:19)

*Questions for Discussion*

1. The people of Judah seemed to be considerably more God-fearing than the people of Israel. Why do you think this was so?
2. Jehu did many good things. Wherein did he fail?
3. Even though Jehu failed to please the Lord in his reign,

how did the Lord show His approval of Jehu's more commendable acts?
4. Why was Elisha displeased when Joash struck the ground
only three times?

*Program Leader*

It might seem strange that though the Kingdom of Judah was
smaller and weaker than the Kingdom of Israel it endured many
years after Israel had fallen. Attempts could be made to explain
this situation according to military and political factors, but the
real reason was that Israel rejected God more completely than
Judah did.

(Closing Prayer)

# 26. Two Good Kings and a Dying Nation

Scripture: II Kings 22:14-20

Suggested Hymns:

> "My Faith Looks Up to Thee"
> "He Leadeth Me, O Blessed Thought"
> "Guide Me, O Thou Great Jehovah"

*Suggestions to Program Leader*

(This program is based on II Kings 18-25. Ask the young people to read these chapters, if possible, before coming to the program. Read the Study Questions, one by one, to the whole group, and let the young people find the answers in their Bibles. The first person who locates the answer should be allowed to give it. When all the Study Questions have been answered, take up the Discussion Questions, encouraging as many people as possible to contribute their ideas.)

*Program Leader's Introduction*

Although Judah was much smaller and weaker than Israel, it survived many years longer as a separate nation. This would not have been possible without God's singular protection of the tiny kingdom. There was good reason for this marked difference between Israel and Judah. Israel was founded on disobedience and disloyalty to the Lord. Israel's first king, Jeroboam, was an able man with a marvelous opportunity, but he set up centers of worship contrary to God's will and encouraged the people in the practice of idolatry. Judah was far from being morally and spiritually perfect, but the smaller nation remained much more loyal to worship as God had prescribed it. Judah was blessed with at least some God-fearing kings. Hezekiah and Josiah were outstanding examples of these. Israel never had the advantage of such leaders. Seen in this light, it is not surprising that the Lord allowed Judah to stand many years after Israel was destroyed.

Even with the good influence of such leaders as Hezekiah and Josiah, there was a consistent decline in Judah's spirituality.

The people seemed much more ready to follow their leadership when it was bad than when it was good. The inevitable result of this growing disloyalty and disobedience was punishment and the destruction of the kingdom.

### Study Questions

1. How old was Hezekiah when he came to the throne and how long did he reign?
2. How did Hezekiah compare with the kings before him and those who followed him with respect to trust in the Lord?
3. Who was reigning in Judah when Israel was overcome by Assyria?
4. What did Rabshakeh say about Judah's trust in the Lord?
5. What did Hezekiah say about the threat of the Assyrians?
6. What did Hezekiah do when he received a threatening letter from the Assyrians?
7. For whose sake did God say He would defend the city of Jerusalem?
8. What befell the Assyrians who beseiged Jerusalem?
9. What medicine was used for Hezekiah's boil?
10. What sign did the Lord give that Hezekiah would be healed from his sickness and that his life would be prolonged?
11. What foolish thing did Hezekiah do when he received a visit from the Babylonians?
12. What was the name of Hezekiah's wife?
13. How did Manasseh compare with his father?
14. What kind of king was Amon and what became of him?
15. How old was Josiah when he began to reign, and how long did he rule?
16. What did Josiah order to be done in his eighteenth year?
17. What was the word of the prophetess Huldah with regard to the nation and with regard to Josiah himself?
18. Who did Josiah call together to hear the reading of the book of the covenant which had been found in the house of the Lord?
19. What did Josiah do with the vessels which had been made for Baal?
20. What did he do with the altar in Bethel?
21. How and where did Josiah die?

22. What new name did the king of Egypt give Eliakim?
23. How many sons of Josiah served as kings of Judah?
24. How was Zedekiah punished and why?
25. What became of the poorer people of Judah after the kingdom fell to Babylon?
26. Who was made governor of the land after the captivity, and what became of him?
27. What did Evil-merodach do to Jehoiachin?

## Questions for Discussion

1. It has been said that the reformations under Hezekiah and Josiah did not go very deep in the life of the people. Do you think this is true or not? Why?
2. Do you think there was something selfish about Hezekiah's statement in II Kings 20:19? Why or why not?
3. Why did it prove a poor policy for God's people to try to establish alliances with their godless neighbor nations?
4. Why was it a mistake for Hezekiah to show the visitors from Babylon all the treasures of his house?

### Program Leader

The merciful and longsuffering nature of God is nowhere seen more clearly than in His dealing with the Kingdom of Judah. Even though times of national repentance were isolated and relatively shallow, God forgave the unfaithfulness of the people again and again and protected the nation against powerful enemies. We can be sure that the same God will be equally generous with us, if we will put our trust in Him and walk in His ways.

(Closing Prayer)

# 27. A Faithful Scribe

Scripture: Jeremiah 29:10-14 and Ezra 1:1-4

Suggested Hymns:

"I Gave My Life for Thee"
"Breathe on Me, Breath of God"
"I Love Thy Kingdom, Lord"

*Suggestions to Program Leader*
(Distribute paper and pencils. Ask the young people, using their own Bibles, to find and write out answers to the Study Questions given below. Ask them to indicate chapter and verse references where the answers were found. When they have completed their work, review the questions and compare the answers that have been given. After this has been done, move on to a consideration of the Discussion Questions.)

*Program Leader's Introduction*
The Bible books of Ezra, Nehemiah, and Esther have to do with the same general period of time in the history of God's people. Ezra and Nehemiah deal with Jews who returned to Jerusalem, and Esther has to do with some of those who were still in the land of captivity.

Ezra was a priest and a scribe who was descended from Zadok and Phinehas. According to the reckoning of the scholars, he was commissioned in 458 or 457 B.C. by the Persian King to lead a group of Jewish captives back to Jerusalem. It appears that another group had returned previously, but had not rebuilt the temple or really restored the worship of God in any adequate way. This rebuilding of the temple and the restoration of worship were the chief tasks which Ezra and his people undertook. Their work was hindered by the laziness and selfishness of some of the citizens and by actual opposition of their enemies. Ezra was not discouraged by the difficulties, and the people experienced a spiritual revival. The book of Ezra gives special emphasis to these two basic tasks, the rebuilding of the house of God and the re-establishment of true worship.

*Questions for Study*

1. What provision was made for the support of the pilgrims returning to Jerusalem in their travels and for their task of building?
2. What valuable possessions which had previously been taken away from the Jews did Cyrus restore at this time?
3. What was the total number of people, including servants, who returned to Jerusalem from the land of captivity at this time?
4. What was the particular feast that was first kept after these exiles returned to Jerusalem?
5. In what year and month did Zerubbabel begin work on the temple?
6. What did the enemies of Judah and Benjamin propose, and how did Zerubbabel respond to their proposal?
7. What was the accusation made against the people of Jerusalem in the letter written by their enemies to the King of Persia? How did the King receive the letter, and what did he order to be done?
8. What decree did the people of Jerusalem ask Darius to look into, and what was the result?
9. In which year and month was the temple completed?
10. How many animals were offered at the dedication of the temple?
11. What were the three things Ezra "prepared his heart" to do?
12. Why did Ezra proclaim a fast at the river of Ahava?
13. What were the sins of the priests and Levites that were reported to Ezra?
14. What did Schechaniah propose to be done with the pagan wives of the people?
15. When all the people were gathered into Jerusalem, what did Ezra call on them to do?

*Questions for Discussion*

1. Do you think the returned exiles delayed unnecessarily in the matter of rebuilding the temple? (See Haggai 1:1-4).

Why was it important that God's house should be rebuilt as quickly as possible?

2. Do you think the bad conduct of the religious leaders (priests and Levites) had anything to do with the slowness of the people to rebuild the temple? Why?

3. What is the value of dedicated leadership in the spiritual life of people today?

4. What were the characteristics which qualified Ezra as an able leader?

*Program Leader*

Too many of the citizens of Jerusalem were more interested in their own comforts than they were in the honor of God and the rebuilding of the temple. This attitude made Ezra's work much more difficult. Without question, the influence of the church is weak today for the same basic reason: too many church members are willing to give to the Lord of their time and their money only after they have satisfied their own desires.

(Closing Prayer)

# 28. An Effective Leader

Scripture: Nehemiah 1

Suggested Hymns:

"Rise Up, O Men of God"
"Stand Up, Stand Up for Jesus"
"Lead On, O King Eternal"

*Suggestions to Program Leader*
(You may conduct this program as a contest. Divide the young people into two groups. Be sure that all have Bibles, preferably their own. Read the study questions, one at a time, and award a point to the side whose representative responds first with the correct answer. You, as program leader, will need to have looked up the answers before the program as a part of your preparation so you will be able to judge correctly when the young people give their answers. It will help a great deal if you will have the answers written out. After the contest, consider the discussion questions, and be sure to allow sufficient time to talk about them.)

*Program Leader's Introduction*
The Book of Nehemiah gives us one of the finest illustrations of effective leadership to be found in the Bible, and Christians who study it thoughtfully always find it interesting and helpful.

Nehemiah had attained a place of great prominence in the land of his captivity. He was cupbearer for the Persian King. His own personal position of favor brought him little satisfaction when he remembered the sad plight of Jerusalem, the city of his fathers. The first returned exiles, who had gone back to Jerusalem about eighty-five years earlier, had not done much to rebuild the city. Nehemiah was greatly distressed when he heard reports of the dilapidated condition of the city walls and gates. With the permission and encouragement of the Persian King, he set out with a group of exiles to return to Jerusalem and to rebuild the walls. The book records not only Nehemiah's success in rebuilding the city but even more importantly his leadership, along with that of Ezra, in spiritual revival among the people.

*Study Questions*

1. What was the condition of the wall and gates of Jerusalem as it was reported to Nehemiah?
2. Who did Nehemiah say had sinned?
3. What did the king notice about Nehemiah's appearance?
4. What were three things Nehemiah asked of the king?
5. What did Nehemiah do at night after he had returned to Jerusalem?
6. Who were the three men who despised Nehemiah and his workers?
7. Were the tribes and families made responsible for repairing sections of the wall nearest to their homes, or was there any designation at all as to where they should work?
8. How weak did Tobiah say the wall would be?
9. Why did the people of Judah say they would not be able to complete the work of rebuilding the wall?
10. What provisions did the builders make to defend themselves and their work against their enemies?
11. In what ways were some of the Jews wronging some of their poorer neighbors?
12. What reply did Nehemiah make when Sanballat and Geshem invited him to a conference?
13. Of what did Sanballat accuse Nehemiah in a letter?
14. Who was the prophet hired by Sanballat and Tobiah?
15. When was the wall completed?
16. What was the number of the congregation in Jerusalem not counting servants?
17. What did Ezra read to the congregation?
18. How long did the people keep the feast?
19. In Chapter 9 it is written of God: "Thou hast done right. . . ." What word is used to characterize the conduct of the people?
20. What did the people promise with regard to the marriages of their sons and daughters?
21. How were the people chosen who were to live in Jerusalem?

22. Who were given charge of "the business of the house of God"?
23. Who was brought into Jerusalem to help keep the dedication of the wall?
24. What three tithes did all Judah bring to the treasury?
25. Why could some of the Jew's children not speak the Jewish language?

## Questions for Discussion

1. What evidences and results of selfishness among the people of Jerusalem did Nehemiah find?
2. Would you say that Nehemiah was a spiritual man? Why?
3. What good "psychology" did Nehemiah use in designating that each family should repair sections of the wall nearest to their houses?
4. What are the evidences that Nehemiah was an effective leader?

### Program Leader

It is a commendable thing when a man is more concerned about the physical and spiritual welfare of his friends and neighbors than he is about his own circumstances. Nehemiah was such a man. How many of us are so unselfish that we sorrow for our friends however comfortable our own circumstances may be? Any person who really has the mind of Christ cannot be fully satisfied as long as the Lord's name is not honored and so long as His people are suffering.

(Closing Prayer)

# 29. A Brave Queen

Scripture: Esther 4

Suggested Hymns:

"God Moves in a Mysterious Way"
"He Leadeth Me, O Blessed Thought"
"There's a Wideness in God's Mercy"

*Suggestions for Program Leader*
(Ask the young people to read the book of Esther before coming to the meeting. Ask the study questions one by one to the whole group and see how many of them the young people can answer without referring to their Bibles. After you have asked all the questions, review them with Bibles open. When you have completed your work with these study questions, take up the discussion questions one by one, allowing the whole group to give their answers and comments.)

*Program Leader's Introduction*
The events described in the Book of Esther took place during the time of Ezra, about 464-385 B.C. Many of the Jews had returned from captivity to Jerusalem, but many others still lived in Persia, the land of their captivity. Esther and Mordecai were among these latter ones. The Persian King, called Ahasuerus, is thought to be the same as the one called Xerxes in other writings. Detailed descriptions of Persian customs in the book reveal that its author was very familiar with the land. This is not, as some people have claimed, a made-up story. The King is known from other sources to have been cruel and given to quick, unwise decisions, even as the Book of Esther describes him.

The Book of Esther has been criticized because the name of God is not to be found in it. It would be foolish to say, however, that there is no evidence of faith in the book. The whole interesting record is a most clear illustration of God's sovereign care of His people. God's name is not to be found in the Book of Esther, but He is there!

*Study Questions*

1. In what condition was Ahasuerus when he ordered his servants to bring Vashti for his guests to admire?
2. What extensive wrong (to all the people) did Memucan say Vashti had done?
3. What was Vashti's punishment?
4. What plan was followed to choose a new queen?
5. What was the blood relation between Esther and Mordecai?
6. What special favor did Mordecai do for the king?
7. What was the position to which the king promoted Haman?
8. Why was Haman angry with Mordecai?
9. What was the decree which Haman asked of the king involving the Jews?
10. When Mordecai learned of Haman's plot, what did he call on Esther to do?
11. When the king received Esther what was the first request she made?
12. Why was Haman so elated about the invitation to attend Esther's banquet?
13. What advice did Haman's wife and friends give with regard to dealing with Mordecai?
14. What did the king discover concerning Mordecai on the night when he could not sleep?
15. When Ahasuerus asked Haman for advice about honoring a man, whom did Haman think he had in mind?
16. What was done to honor Mordecai, and who carried out the king's command to do it?
17. What warning did Haman's wife and friends give him when they heard about the honoring of Mordecai?
18. Why did the king leave Esther's feast and go out into the garden?
19. What became of Haman?
20. What was done for Mordecai?
21. How did the king manage to counteract the order he had given for the destruction of the Jews?
22. What is the name of the feast which commemorates the deliverance of the Jews in the time of Esther?

## Questions for Discussion

1. Although the name of God is not mentioned in the Book of Esther, what evidences of faith are to be found in Esther and Mordecai?

2. "All things work together for good to them that love God, to them who are the called according to His purpose." Mention incidents from the book which illustrate this truth.

3. What special examples of courage are to be found in the book?

4. What do you think of the method which was followed to choose a new queen?

5. Do you think Vashti was justified in her decision? Why?

*Program Leader*

It is not easy for us to understand how much courage was required for Esther to do what she did. We are totally unfamiliar with the kind of complete, terrifying power which the king of Persia exercised over all his subjects, including his wives. How many of us would be willing to risk our security and even our lives for the sake of our family and friends? We hope that we are never faced with such a situation, but let us pray that God will give us courage to do whatever is right and honorable under any and all circumstances.

(Closing Prayer)

# 30. The Birth and Early Life of the Saviour

Scripture: Luke 2:1-20

Suggested Hymns:

"Thou Didst Leave Thy Throne"
"It Came Upon the Midnight Clear"
"Joy to the World"

## Suggestions to Program Leader

(To present this program, you may use a panel of three or four people who have been chosen beforehand. Ask the panel members and the other young people, too, to read Luke 1 through 4:13 very carefully before coming to the meeting. Seat the panel members around the table before the other young people. Address the questions to those on the panel in turn. When the person to whom the question is given has had full opportunity to answer, let the other panel members make their contributions. At the conclusion of the program, invite all the young people to raise questions and make comments.)

## Program Leader's Introduction

For the first thirty years after Christ's death and resurrection, the good news about Jesus was transmitted almost altogether by word of mouth. There were many eye-witnesses who could be appealed to as authorities. As the church grew in numbers and in area, and, as the eye-witnesses began to disappear from the scene, the need for a written record became increasingly apparent. It was then that the Holy Spirit inspired the Gospel writers to set down what Jesus "began both to do and to teach."

The Gospels tell about the life of Jesus, but they are not biographies, properly speaking. They give biographical information, to be sure, but their main purpose is to present Christ as Saviour and Lord, and to urge people to believe on Him.

Luke was a very able and careful historian. His Gospel is the longest book in the New Testament in number of words, and goes into greater detail than the other Gospels. In the introduction of his Gospel, Luke states that his purpose is to give an accurate, orderly account of the things of Christ, so that those people who were being instructed in Christianity might know the "certainty" of the things they were being taught. Jesus is presented as the Lord of all, and as the Saviour of mankind. This Gospel is especially appropriate for, and appealing to, Gentile readers.

As we shall see in our study, the opening chapters of Luke set forth most clearly the divine origin of Christ, the miracle of His birth, and the preparations for His work. As we read once more these words which are so familiar and so rich in beauty, it is easy to see why Luke has been called "the most beautiful book in the world."

## Study Questions

1. What makes it seem likely that other records of the life and ministry of Jesus were in existence when Luke began to write his Gospel?

2. What indication is there that Luke had contact with people who had been closely and personally associated with Jesus?

3. Why do you think Luke began his Gospel with an account of the birth of John?

4. The meaning of the name John is "the Lord is merciful" or "the [free] gift of God." What significance does this have for the task which John was to fulfill?

5. Why was Zachariah unable to speak for a time?

6. Did the angel's greeting to Mary mean that she would be able to give grace to others (as the Roman Catholic Church teaches), or that she had received the grace of God in a special way?

7. Compare the statements of the angels concerning the greatness of John and the greatness of Jesus. What difference was there?

8. Who sang the first song in honor of the Saviour? (Not the angels.)

9. To what attributes or qualities of God did Mary refer in her song of praise?

10. What did Zachariah say, in his song, would be the work of his son, John?

11. Why did Joseph and Mary go from Nazareth to Bethlehem?

12. In what way was the conduct of the shepherds, as explained in Luke 2:17, a good pattern for all Christians?
13. Since Jesus was born without sin, why was it necessary for the religious ceremonies for infants to be performed on His behalf?
14. What are the first recorded words of Jesus, and what do they reveal about His understanding of who he really was?
15. How is Luke 2:52 a summary of ideal human development?
16. What are the main points in John's message in Chapter 3?
17. Why did Herod imprison John?
18. Why does the Bible say of Jesus, "as was supposed, the son of Joseph"?
19. What is the significance of Jesus' ancestry being traced by Luke all the way to Adam? (See I Corinthians 15: 22, 45)
20. Would you say that Hebrews 4:15 is a good summary and explanation of Luke 4:1-13? Why?

*Program Leader*

A study of the gospel of Jesus Christ is not a mere biographical consideration of a great person of ancient history. Jesus is altogether unique. He is the One whose life and work have completely changed the world. We ourselves should not approach this study in an ordinary way. We should come to it expectantly, asking God to prepare our hearts for a blessing and to make us a blessing to others.

(Closing Prayer)

# 31. The Ministry of Jesus in Galilee

Scripture: Luke 4:14-37

Suggested Hymns:

"O For a Thousand Tongues to Sing"
"What a Friend We Have in Jesus"
"My Faith Looks Up to Thee"

*Suggestions to Program Leader*
(Ask all the young people to study Luke 4:14—9:50 very carefully before they come to the meeting. Distribute paper and pencils to all. Read the questions one by one allowing the young people time to write out the brief answers from memory. When they have completed their answers, review the questions with Bibles open. Let each person check his own answers, then take up the discussion questions with the whole group.)

*Program Leader's Introduction*
The Lord's ministry in Galilee was carried on in an area and among people with whom He was very familiar. Through the things He did and said, He revealed Himself and His will for men. He made it plain that He was the one whom the Old Testament prophets had predicted would come. He revealed His divine authority to teach and to perform miracles, even to the forgiving of sins and the raising of the dead. He accepted the appraisal of the disciples that He was indeed the Christ of God. All these claims were fully authenticated when the approval of the Father was so clearly revealed at the Mount of Transfiguration. The thoughtful study of these chapters will increase our understanding of who Jesus is and of what He came to do.

## Study Questions

1. From which Old Testament book did Jesus read when He went to the synagogue in Nazareth?
2. To whom did He say the prophecy was referring?
3. Whose mother-in-law did Jesus heal of a fever?

4. What did Simon say when Jesus told him and the others to let down their fishing nets?

5. What happened to their nets?

6. What, instead of fish, did Jesus say they would catch from that time on?

7. What did the friends of the palsied man do when they could not get him into the house where Jesus was?

8. What were the Pharisees thinking to themselves when Jesus forgave the man's sins?

9. Complete the statement: "They that are whole need not a physician, but they that . . . . . . . . . . . . . ."

10. Supply the missing word:" I came not to call the righteous, but . . . . . . to repentance."

11. Supply the missing word: "The Son of man is Lord also of the . . . . . . ."

12. Name as many as you can of the apostles.

13. Supply the missing words: "Bless them that . . . . . . you, and . . . . . . for them which despitefully use you."

14. Supply the missing words: "Be ye therefore . . . . . . , as your Father also is . . . . . . ."

15. Supply the missing words: "For a good tree bringeth not forth corrupt . . . . . . ; neither doth a corrupt tree bring forth . . . . . . fruit."

16. Did the centurion who sent to Jesus at Capernaum insist that the Lord should come to his house?

17. What did Jesus do for the son of the widow of Nain?

18. Of whom did Jesus say, "Among those that are born of women there is not a greater prophet than he"?

19. What question did John tell his disciples to ask Jesus?

20. What did Simon the Pharisee think when Jesus allowed the sinful woman to anoint Him?

21. What kind of people are represented by the "thorny ground"?

22. Jesus said that His mother and brethren were those who " . . . . . . the word of God and . . . . . . it."

23. What became of the devils whom Jesus cast out of the man of Gaderea?

24. How old was the daughter of Jairus?

25. What did the mourners do when Jesus said the maiden was asleep.

26. Who did Herod think Jesus might be?

27. How many baskets of fragments were taken up after Jesus had fed the five thousand?
28. When Jesus asked, "Whom say ye that I am?" how did Peter answer?
29. What did Peter propose to build on the Mount of Transfiguration?
30. Supply the missing words: "For he that is ...... among you all, the same shall be ......."

## Questions for Discussion

1. Why were the Pharisees "filled with madness" when Jesus healed a man on the Sabbath day?
2. What did Jeus mean by the "blind leading the blind"?
3. What was the application of the parable in 7:41-42?
4. What did Jesus mean by 9:25?
5. Were the events at the Mount of Transfiguration an indication that the Lord's ministry was approved by the Father? Why?

### Program Leader

Jesus was not satisfied for His disciples merely to know what other people were saying about Him. He wanted them to have a conviction of their own and to be willing to confess it. The same thing is expected of us. It is not enough for us to know about Jesus—we must answer for ourselves as to what we believe. What do you think of Christ? Do you believe that He is the Son of God and Saviour of sinners? Do you trust Him as your own Saviour and Lord, and are you willing to say so publicly?

(Closing Prayer)

# 32. From Galilee to Jerusalem

Scripture: Luke 14:12-24

Suggested Hymns:

"Jesus, the Very Thought of Thee"
"Holy Spirit, Faithful Guide"
"Jesus, I My Cross Have Taken"

*Suggestions to Program Leader*

(For the sake of variety, you may want to conduct part of this program as a contest. By way of preparation, ask the young people to study Luke 9:51—14:35 very carefully before coming to the meeting. Divide the members into two groups. Ask the questions, and recognize the person who first raises his hand indicating that he knows the answer. Award a point to the side whose representative first gives the correct answer. It will make your job as judge and quizmaster easier if you will have the answers to the questions written out before the program begins. After the contest is completed, take up the discussion questions with the whole group.)

*Program Leader's Introduction*

In Luke 9:51 we read of Jesus that "he steadfastly set his face to go to Jerusalem." This trip to Jerusalem was no ordinary journey. The Lord knew why He had come into the world, and He knew what awaited Him at Jerusalem. He knew that He would encounter increasing enmity. He knew that He would be betrayed to His enemies. He knew that He would be paying for the sins of the world with His own sufferings and death. His disciples understood these things very vaguely, if at all. Let us notice, as we read and study these chapters which tell of the Lord's progress toward Jerusalem, how the opposition to Him mounted as time went on. Let us also notice hints of His own consciousness of what was to take place and how He faithfully prepared His disciples for what was to come.

*Study Questions*

1. What did James and John want to do with respect to the Samaritans who would not receive Jesus?
2. Complete the statement: "No man, having put his hand to the plow, and looking back is fit for the . . . . . . . . . . . . . . . . . . . . . . . ."
3. What did Jesus tell the disciples to do when they left a city where they were not received?
4. Who did Jesus say He beheld "as lightning" fall from heaven?
5. How did Jesus answer the lawyer who asked "What shall I do to inherit eternal life"?
6. What method did Jesus use to teach who are to be thought of as our neighbors?
7. To whom did Martha complain when her sister Mary did not help her with preparations for the meal?
8. Why did Jesus say the man should lend bread to his neighbor even though it was not convenient?
9. If men give good things to their children, what will God give to them that ask Him?
10. Through whom did Jesus' enemies say He was casting out devils?
11. Complete the statement: "Blessed are they that hear the . . . . . . . . . . . . . . . . . . . and keep it!"
12. What sign only did Jesus say would be given to those who sought a sign?
13. Supply the missing word: "Be not afraid of them that . . . . . . the body, and after that have no more that they can do."
14. Supply the missing word: "Ye are of more value than many . . . . . . ."
15. What sin did Jesus say would not be forgiven?
16. Complete the statement: "A man's life consisteth not in the abundance of the things which he . . . . . . ."
17. What did God call the man who sought to lay up material goods for his soul?
18. Supply the missing words: "The life is more than . . . . . . , and the body is more than . . . . . . ."

19. Supply the missing words: "Seek ye the ........ ......
........; and all these things shall be added unto you."
20. Supply the missing word: "Where your treasure is, there will your ...... be also."
21. Supply the missing word: "Except ye ......, ye shall all likewise perish."
22. Why did the ruler of the synagogue criticize Jesus for healing the woman with the infirmity?
23. What did Jesus say would be done for people who humbled themselves?
24. What did the master of the house do when his invited guests refused to come to his supper?
25. Why does a man count the cost before he begins to build a tower?

## Questions for Discussion

1. How can the example of the "Good Samaritan" be practically applied in our times?
2. What lesson can we learn from the incident which took place at the home of Martha and Mary? (10:38-42)
3. What is the meaning of 11:24-26?
4. In 11:37-44 a Pharisee criticized Jesus for failing to perform a ceremonial washing before He ate. What is the meaning of Jesus' reply, and how can we apply it to the present?
5. What does 12:13-21 have to say about a materialistic philosophy of life?
6. What was Jesus saying with regard to the Sabbath in 13:11-17?
7. What did Jesus mean by "hating father, mother, wife," etc., in 14:25-27?

### Program Leader

We can learn a valuable lesson by observing the way Christ faced opposition and enmity. He certainly did not go out of His way to invite trouble, but neither did He seek to avoid it when it came. Furthermore, He was never bitter about the undeserved wrongs which He suffered. II Timothy 3:12 says, "All that will live godly in Christ Jesus shall suffer persecution." If we are Christians, we may expect opposition in this life. If we are

Christians, we should also seek to face opposition as our Lord did. With His help, we can.

(Closing Prayer)

# 33. Jesus the Teacher

Scripture:  Luke 15

Suggested Hymns:

"Saviour, Teach Me Day by Day"
"Wonderful Words of Life"
"All the Way My Saviour Leads Me"

## Suggestions to Program Leader

(Supply all the young people with Bibles. If there is time, let them read Luke 15-19:27 before you consider the questions. It would actually be better if they did this reading at home, but if that is not possible it would be profitable for them to do it in the meeting. This program will be an "open Bible" study. Read the questions aloud one by one. Let the young people volunteer the answers when they find them in their Bibles, giving both the answer and the chapter and verse reference. When you come to the discussion questions, be sure to allow ample time for everyone who has an idea to express it.)

## Program Leader's Introduction

Jesus was known to many people in His time as "the Teacher." No part of the Bible gives us a better picture of the beauty and excellence of His teaching ability than the chapters before us in this program (Luke 15—19:27). His words were so plain and simple that the most unlearned could get the meaning of them, and at the same time His ideas were so profound that the wisest and most highly educated people were amazed at Him. The best thing about Jesus' teaching was that it concerned things which are most important to us. He said, "The Son of man is come to seek and to save that which was lost." By His teaching and His life and death, He met the spiritual needs of men and opened the way for the eternal salvation for their souls.

## Study Questions

1. What was the complaint of the Pharisees and Scribes which

led Jesus to give the parables of the lost sheep, the lost coin, and the lost son?

2.  What did the shepherd and the woman call on their neighbors to do after they had found what was lost?

3.  What did the prodigal son say when "he came to himself"?

4.  Why did the prodigal son not finish the speech which he had planned when he came home?

5.  Why was the elder brother angry?

6.  Why did the steward of the rich man lose his job?

7.  How did the steward win the friendship and loyalty of his master's debtors?

8.  What did Jesus say about the steadfastness of the law?

9.  What does the Bible say about the possibility of passing from hell to heaven after death?

10.  Why did Abraham say it would be pointless for one to return from the dead in order to warn the wicked?

11.  What did Jesus say about those through whom offenses come?

12.  What is possible to those who have "faith as a grain of mustard seed"?

13.  What was the nationality of the leper who returned to give thanks for his healing?

14.  Where did Jesus say the kingdom of God was?

15.  Jesus likened the times of His coming to the times of two men in the Old Testament. Who were those two Old Testament characters?

16.  Why did the judge decide to grant the widow's request?

17.  What was the prayer of the publican?

18.  What did Jesus say about permitting little children to come to Him?

19.  What was the one thing the rich young man lacked?

20.  What did Jesus say about the difficulty of the rich entering the kingdom of God?

21.  What did Jesus say would befall him when he arrived at Jerusalem?

22.  What two things did Jesus do for the blind beggar of Jericho?

23.  What did Zacchaeus do in order to see Jesus?

24. What was the complaint of the people because Jesus went to Zacchaeus' house?
25. What instruction did the nobleman give to his servants?

## Discussion Questions

1. In the parable of the prodigal son, what was the difference in the attitudes of the two sons toward their father?
2. What does the account of the rich man and Lazarus have to say about not postponing the decision to receive Christ as Saviour?
3. Do you think the account of the ten lepers is an accurate description of our normal gratitude toward God? Why?
4. What do you think Jesus meant by "receiving the kingdom as a little child"?
5. What does the incident involving Zacchaeus have to say about Christ's concern for outcasts?

### Program Leader

Still today a great many people admire Jesus as a teacher even though they are not willing to believe in Him as Saviour and Lord. This is a rather unreasonable position, is it not? If Jesus is truly a great teacher, we ought to believe what He said and be obedient to His teachings. He said that He was the Son of God and the Saviour of the world. If we really admire Him and respect His teachings, then we must believe in Him and trust our lives to Him.

(Closing Prayer)

# 34. The Death and Resurrection of the Saviour

Scripture: Luke 23:33-47; 24:1-9

Suggested Hymns:

"Beneath the Cross of Jesus"
"When I Survey the Wondrous Cross"
"The Head That Once Was Crowned with Thorns"

*Suggestions to Program Leader*

(Ask your young people to read and study Luke 19:28 through 24:53 very carefully before coming to the meeting. Distribute paper and pencils to all. Read the study questions one by one and let the young people write out their answers. When all have finished, have them open their Bibles for a review of the questions. Let each person check his own paper. When you have finished checking answers to the study questions, ask the discussion questions one by one and give ample opportunity for every young person to make his contribution.)

*Program Leader's Introduction*

The death and resurrection of Jesus Christ are at the very heart of the gospel. That is why all the Gospel writers devote so large a portion of their writings to a description of the last days of the Lord's earthly ministry.

In the clear, detailed words of a skilled historian, Luke gives us an account of Christ's sufferings, trial, death, and resurrection. He is careful to give the exact names of persons and places. He mentions the exact hours of the day. All of these details assure us of the genuineness of his report. Luke, though, is concerned with more than accuracy of details. He is concerned with the meaning of Christ's death and resurrection, for it is by means of His death and resurrection that the Lord is able "to seek and to save that which was lost."

## Study Questions

1. What did the disciples answer when the owners asked, "Why loose ye the colt?"
2. What did Jesus say would immediately have cried out if the people had kept silent?
3. Supply the missing words: "My house is the house of . . . . . . but ye have made it a den of . . . . . . ."
4. What did the leaders of the Jews reply when Jesus asked if the baptism of John were from heaven or of men?
5. In the parable of the vineyard, who did the son of the owner represent?
6. Supply the missing words: "Render unto Caesar the things which be . . . . . . . ., and unto . . . . . . . . the things which be . . . . . . . . ."
7. In the story told by the Sadducees to question the resurrection, how many husbands did the woman have?
8. From which book of the Old Testament did Jesus take this quotation: "The LORD said unto my Lord, sit thou on my right hand till I make thine enemies thy footstool"?
9. How much did the poor widow cast into the treasury?
10. Supply the missing word: "Ye shall be . . . . . . . . of all men for my name's sake."
11. Supply the missing word: "Heaven and earth shall pass away, but . . . . . . . . . . . . shall not pass away."
12. What was the name of the feast of unleavened bread?
13. What was the man carrying whom Peter and John followed to the house where they would eat the passover?
14. To whom did Jesus say: "Satan hath desired to have you that he may sift you as wheat"?
15. What did Peter do when he realized that he had denied Jesus?
16. Why did Pilate send Jesus to Herod?
17. Who hoped to see Jesus perform a miracle?
18. Who was the prisoner who was released to the people?
19. Complete the words of Jesus to the penitent thief: "Today thou shalt be with me in . . . . . . ."
20. What happened in the temple when Jesus died?
21. What did the Centurion say when Jesus died?

22. Which one of the disciples went to the sepulcher after he had heard the report of the resurrection from the women?
23. Give the name of one of the two people from Emmaus.
24. What did Jesus eat when he appeared to the disciples?
25. Where did Jesus tell the disciples to wait until they received power from on high?

## Discussion Questions

1. Why were the chief priests and the scribes so disturbed about the parable recorded in Luke 20:9-18?
2. How did Jesus use himself as an example to teach the meaning of true greatness?
3. What evidences does Luke give of Pilate's weakness?
4. Why can it be said that Joseph of Arimathaea's action called for love and courage?
5. What evidence does Luke give that the Lord's resurrection body was real and material and not merely a ghost or a vision?

### Program Leader

Christianity is a unique religion. Other religions have had wide followings, wise teachers, and honored leaders. Christianity stands alone in having a leader and founder who is God Himself and who suffered and died in place of sinful men in order that they might be forgiven and receive everlasting life. We must never allow our eyes of faith to be turned away from the cross and the empty tomb. These events are basic to the uniqueness of our faith.

(Closing Prayer)

# 35. The Church Founded

Scripture: Acts 1:1-11

Suggested Hymns:

> "I Love Thy Kingdom, Lord"
> "Come, Holy Spirit, Heavenly Dove"
> "I Love to Tell the Story"

*Suggestions to Program Leader*

(You may conduct the question and answer part of this program as a contest. As a part of your own preparation, look up and write out the answers to the fact questions before coming to the meeting. Ask the young people to read Acts 1-7 very carefully beforehand, since they will be answering the questions from memory. Following the "Leader's Introduction," divide the group into two teams. Ask the questions to the teams, in turn, going down the line, first to one team and then to the other, until the right answer is given. Award a point to the side giving the correct answer, and then go on to the next person on the next team. Appoint someone to keep score. When all the study questions are answered, take up the discussion questions with the whole group.)

*Program Leader's Introduction*

The Book of Acts is sometimes called "The Acts of the Holy Spirit." When we read the book carefully, it is easy to see why this is so—the name of the Holy Spirit is repeated over and over, and He is very obviously the moving force behind all that takes place. His activity in the church is in answer to Christ's promise that He would come.

Acts gives a thrilling account of the early years of the church as we know it. It is a mistake to think that God was without a people before this time. There is a real sense in which the church of God existed in the Old Testament era, but it was at this particular point that it was transformed from a national to a worldwide body. As Acts 1:8 says, it began in Jerusalem, overflowed into Judea and Samaria, and was and is being extended to the "uttermost part of the earth." It is by this gracious extension of the church to all peoples that Gentile Christians are included, and how very grateful we should be. If we are indeed grateful, we can prove our gratitude by carrying out Christ's commission to tell others.

## Study Questions

1. Where did Jesus tell the apostles to wait until they received the Holy Spirit?
2. How did Jesus answer when the apostles asked if He were going to restore the kingdom to Israel at that time?
3. What did the men in white apparel say about the coming again of Christ?
4. How was a successor to Judas chosen?
5. What were the sounds and sights which accompanied the coming of the Holy Spirit?
6. How did the mockers explain the ability of the apostles to speak in different tongues?
7. Who gave the real explanation of what had taken place, and to which prophet did he refer?
8. About how many people were there who believed and were baptized on the day of Pentecost?
9. Where were Peter and John going when they came upon the lame man?
10. What did Peter say to the man when he asked them for money?
11. By whose name and whose power did Peter say the healing of the lame man had taken place?
12. What special thing about Peter's message offended the Saducees?
13. What was done to Peter and John at this time?
14. After the hearing was held, what did the Jewish rulers demand of Peter and John, and how did they answer?
15. Who was the man who sold his land and gave the money to the apostles?
16. Who were the people who sold land in order to make a gift, but who lied about the amount they received?
17. What became of these two?

18. How did the apostles escape after they had been imprisoned by the chief priest?
19. What was Gamaliel's advice to the Jews?
20. Why did the apostles rejoice after they had been beaten?
21. Why did the Greek Christians complain against the Hebrew Christians?
22. How many men were chosen to "serve tables"?
23. What was the charge which Stephen's accusers brought against him?
24. What did the Jews do to Stephen?
25. Who kept the clothes of the men who did the stoning?
26. Who did Stephen see before he died?
27. What was Stephen's prayer for his persecutors?

## Questions for Discussion

1. What evidence is there in Luke 1:3 and Acts 1:1 that Luke was the author of Acts?
2. What were the main points in the preaching of the apostles?
3. Why do you think the early Christian preachers made so many references to the Old Testament?
4. In what locality did most of the events recorded in Chapters 1-7 take place?

*Program Leader*

There is no question about the successfulness of the work of the apostles during the very early days of the Christian church. What was the secret of their success? They were faithful to proclaim Jesus as the Son of God who was crucified and risen. They called on men to repent of their sins and to believe in Christ for salvation, and they trusted in the power of the Holy Spirit to work through them.

(Closing Prayer)

# 36. The Church Scattered

Scripture: Acts 11:1-18

Suggested Hymns:

> "In the Hour of Trial"
> "My Hope Is Built on Nothing Less"
> "Jesus, Keep Me Near the Cross"

*Suggestions to Program Leader*

(This program may be conducted as a panel discussion. You, as leader, will be moderator of the panel. Choose three or four young people to serve as panel members. Ask them to read Chapters 8-12 very carefully in preparation for the program. The other young people would do well to read these chapters also. Both those who are on the panel and those who are not may use their Bibles during the program. Assemble the panel around a table so all the members will be facing the group. When you have given the "Leader's Introduction," address the questions one by one to panel members. When the person to whom the question is addressed has completed his answer, ask the other panel members for their comments.)

*Program Leader's Introduction*

As we discovered in our first program on the Book of Acts, the opposition to Christianity in Jerusalem became very violent. This violence reached its height when the leaders of the Jews stoned Stephen to death, but this was not the end of the persecution. Not only were Christian teachers and leaders in danger for their lives, but anyone who believed in and worshipped Jesus was under the shadow of death. It became impossible to preach Jesus openly. We might think this persecution in Jerusalem would have meant the death of the Christian church, but it was not to be that way at all. Jesus had told His followers to go out from Jerusalem into the other cities and town of Judea and even into Samaria. Following the persecution in Jerusalem, they did just that—they went to other communities of Judea and into Samaria. It was not an accident. The Bible tells us that the Lord sent them forth, and Chapters 8-12 tell of what took place.

*Questions*

1.  What evidences are there that Philip's ministry in Samaria produced results?

2.  What serious mistake did Simon of Samaria make, and why do you think he wanted power to bestow the Holy Spirit on people?

3.  What factors made the Ethiopian eunuch so receptive to the Good News about Christ?

4.  What caused Saul, the Pharisee, to seek the aid of the high priest, and why was it strange that he should do so?

5.  Saul thought he had been persecuting heretics, but who was it that he was really persecuting?

6.  Would you say that Ananias was a man of great faith? Why?

7.  How was the generosity of Barnabas demonstrated in his dealing with Paul?

8.  What factor made the friends of Dorcas especially distressed when she died?

9.  How long after Cornelius' vision was it that Peter received the message of God through a trance, and how does this timing demonstrate the providence of God?

10. What was the real meaning of the message Peter received through the trance, and how did he apply it practically?

11. How did the Jewish Christians of Jerusalem receive the news that Peter had baptized believers who were not Jews, and how did Peter answer them?

12. Who was sent to minister to the believers at Antioch, what were the believers called, and who did the new minister seek to be his associate there?

13. When did Peter really understand that he was being miraculously delivered from prison?

14. How do verses 23 and 24 of Chapter 12 illustrate that God's enemies, however powerful they may seem to be, are powerless to hinder the word and work of God?

*Program Leader*

In these chapters we have been studying, a fundamental development was the acceptance into the church of believers who were not originally Jews. At this time it was recognized openly that it was God's purpose to save the world, not merely the people of one nation, through the redeeming work of Christ.

Another significant development is that Peter is not heard of in the Book of Acts after the words in 12:17, "and he departed and went into another place." A new leader was already on the scene in the person of Paul. This merely illustrates the fact that the work of spreading the gospel is God's, and does not depend on any one man for its success.

(Closing Prayer)

# 37. The Church Extended

Scripture:  Acts 13:44-52

Suggested Hymns:

"Jesus, Thou Joy of Loving Hearts"
"Love Divine, All Loves Excelling"
"Lead On, O King Eternal"

*Suggestions to Program Leader*
(This is a program in which all of your young people will be better prepared if they will read Acts 13-20 before coming to the meeting. Ask the questions orally one by one. Let the person indicate by the raised hand that he has located the answer in his Bible. Then let him give the answer and the chapter and verse reference where it was found. If the answer given first is not correct, recognize someone else. This procedure will make it necessary that you, as program leader, will have found and written out the answers together with references before beginning the program. When all of the study questions have been answered, take up the discussion questions, allowing ample time for comments and additional questions about each one.)

*Program Leader's Introduction*
The chapters from Acts included in this part of our study (13-20) describe one of the most thrilling periods in the history of the Christian church. It was at this time that the powerful message of Jesus Christ moved out into the world, and, as some observed, "turned the world upside down." There could be no doubt of the genuineness of what was taking place. Those who received Christ by faith did not merely pretend to be changed. They were really, radically transformed from evil people to good people, from darkness to light, from death to life.

That the work was the Lord's was also obvious. It was not a mere human program and campaign. Had it been only this it could not have succeeded. The workers, though dedicated, were too few. They had no wealth or organization. They faced bitter and determined opposition on every hand. The only explanation

114

for the phenomenal growth of the early church among the Gentiles is that it was the work—the acts—of God's Holy Spirit working through men who were faithful to exalt Jesus Christ as Son of God and Saviour.

### Study Questions

1. Who said, "Separate me Barnabas and Saul"?
2. Of what sin was Elymas guilty and what was his punishment?
3. In which Psalm and which verse is it written, "Thou art my Son, this day have I begotten Thee"?
4. Who was it that "brought" Paul and Barnabas to give the message of salvation again on the following Sabbath?
5. Who did the people of Lystra think Paul and Barnabas were?
6. How did Paul say God witnessed to people who had not heard the message of God in words?
7. Who caused Paul to be stoned at Lystra?
8. Who "opened the door of faith unto the Gentiles"?
9. How did Peter say that both Jews and Gentiles would be saved?
10. Why did Paul not want to take Mark with him and Barnabas on their second journey?
11. What happened to the partnership of Barnabas and Paul, and who became Paul's new companion?
12. Of what nationalities were Timothy's parents?
13. What prompted Paul to take the gospel into Macedonia?
14. Why were the masters of the girl with the spirit angry with Paul and Silas?
    Were they really concerned about their teachings?
15. Why was the prison keeper about to kill himself?
16. What did the jailer ask, and how did Paul and Silas answer him?
17. Where did Paul preach first in Thessalonica according to his custom?
18. What unintentioned compliment did the rulers of Thessalonica pass on Paul and Silas?
19. Why is it written that the people of Berea were "more noble"?

20. Who stirred up the people at Berea?
21. At what point in Paul's message did some of the Athenians mock?
22. With whom did Paul live in Corinth, and what was their occupation?
23. Who said, "I have much people in this city," and what was the city in question?
24. Who instructed Apollos more perfectly in the way of Christ?
25. Where were the believers who had not heard of the Holy Ghost?
26. What two things disturbed Demetrius about the teaching of Paul, and in what order did he mention them?
27. What was the name of the young man who went to sleep while Paul was preaching, and what happened to him?
28. Where was Paul when he sent for the elders from Ephesus?
29. What did Paul say he had not shunned to declare?
30. Why did the people weep at Paul's departure from Miletus?

## Discussion Questions

1. Why is there the change from the third person "they" in Acts 16:8 to the first person "we" in Acts 16:10?
2. In his sermon at Athens, how did Paul make use of his knowledge of the literature and thought of the Greeks?
3. What did Demetrius have in common with the masters of the slave girl in Philippi as to motives?

### Program Leader

As we noted at the beginning of this study, God honored and blessed the work of those who trusted in the power of the Spirit and who proclaimed Christ faithfully. We believe He still honors and blesses such faith and proclamation today. What are some concrete evidences that He does?

(Closing Prayer)